CAPTIVE

CAPTIVE

2,147 DAYS OF TERROR IN THE COLOMBIAN JUNGLE

CLARA ROJAS

TRANSLATED BY ADRIANA V. LÓPEZ

ATRIA PAPERBACK

NEW YORK LONDON TORONTO SYDNEY

ATRIA PAPERBACK
A Division of Simon & Schuster, Inc.
1230 Avenue of the Americas
New York, NY 10020

I particularly thank Isabel García-Zarza for her help in the drafting of this work.

Captive copyright © 2009 by PLON
Originally published in France as *Captive* in 2009 by PLON
Published by arrangement with PLON

First Atria Paperback edition May 2010

ATRIA PAPERBACK and colophon are trademarks
of Simon & Schuster, Inc.

For information about special discounts for bulk purchases,
please contact Simon & Schuster Special Sales at
1-866-506-1949 or business@simonandschuster.com.

The Simon & Schuster Speakers Bureau can bring authors to your live event.
For more information or to book an event contact the Simon & Schuster Speakers
Bureau at 1-866-248-3049 or visit our website at www.simonspeakers.com.

Manufactured in the United States of America

10 9 8 7 6 5 4 3 2 1

Library of Congress Cataloging-in-Publication Data
Rojas, Clara.
   [Cautiva. English]
   Captive : 2,147 days of terror in the Colombian jungle / Clara Rojas ; translated
from the Spanish by Adriana V. López.
       p. cm.
    1. Rojas, Clara—Kidnapping, 2002.   2. Rojas, Clara—Captivity, 2002–2009.
3. Hostages—Colombia—Biography.   4. Mothers and daughters—Colombia—
Biography.   5. Fuerzas Armadas Revolucionarias de Colombia.   I. Adriana V.
López.   II. Title.
   HV6604.C72R65713 2010
   364.15'4092—dc22
   [B]   2009049229
ISBN 978-1-4391-5695-7
ISBN 978-1-4391-7609-2 (ebook)

Contents

CONTENTS

CAPTIVE

1

Dispatched from Freedom

JULY 22, 2008

It's been almost six months now that I have been free, and it still feels like it's all a dream. Early each morning, I awake to the sound of birds chirping all around me. I live in Bogotá's savanna, where the air is crisp and I can take in the mountain scenery from my window. There isn't a morning that goes by that I don't thank God I'm still alive. It's the first thing I do upon opening my eyes. Yes, to thank the blessing that's re-united me with my mother, with my son, Emmanuel, with my family and friends, and with all those who I love most. I am grateful to finally be able to leave it all behind. The kidnap-ping, the captivity—that's all in the past. Now that my life is back to normal, with the affection and company of my loved ones, it's strange to recall that not so long ago, when I was rotting away in the jungle, I could have felt so alone. So utterly forgotten.

Many have asked if I've changed since the kidnapping; if I'm still the same Clara that I always was. I tell them yes, that for the most part, I'm still the same person—but with a scar on my stomach now, and a profound mark made on the way I think and feel about things, which I can only hope will fade with time. Sometimes I'm assaulted by feelings of sadness, but, luckily, I have Emmanuel at my side for comfort. As is expected, I would have preferred that the Colombian guerrilla organization known as the FARC hadn't robbed me of six years of my life. But I'm alive and here to tell the tale. Each person will recount what the war was like from his or her perspective. I'm just another soldier. And this is my story.

These words come from the depths of my heart, and I write this for many reasons. First, I've always dreamed of writing a book. I've written various academic and professional works, but this is a chance to bare my soul in the world of letters, a field that I've always adored. I'm also inspired to write a memoir so that it remains for my son and those of his generation. Because I long to be part of a country that prioritizes reconciliation, forgiveness, tolerance, growth, and peace. Lastly, I want to share my experience with readers and have them understand the difficulties I suffered and overcame, so that perhaps while reading this book, a seed of hope and longing will be planted in their hearts.

2

My Mother

Before delving into my story, I first want to express what a tremendous gift my mother has been to me.

I've been rewarded with many things in my life, but my mother is, without a doubt, one of the greatest blessings. How can I not thank God for her existence, wisdom, tenacity, energy, and tremendous generosity? It seems like it was only yesterday that I was crying in the wilderness, clinging to a barbwire fence, demanding that they set me free. I yearned to be close to my *mamita*, I missed her so much, and I sensed her weakened, distressed, and needing me close.

When I think of my time without her, I always remember this moment: it was sometime in early May 2006, about six in the evening as it was starting to get dark, when the guerrilla commander holding us captive ordered us to call everyone together. He approached me with a magazine in his hands and said, "Look, there's your mother. So you can see for yourself she's fine. Maybe now you can let go of that fence you've been clutching on to. We're up to fucking here with your tantrums!" He handed me a copy of *Semana*, a respected Colombian news magazine in the tradition of *Time*. On the cover was a picture of my mother with the accompanying headline "If my daughter gave birth in the jungle, I want to hold the baby in my arms." I ran off to my hammock and closed the mosquito net around me, crying my eyes out; I don't think I even thanked him for the magazine. A little while later, one of my fellow captives came over to tell me that I should read the article fast, because it was meant for everyone, and I'd have to give it back.

Then I overheard a similar complaint from another captive. I couldn't understand why anyone else would find the article of interest and why they wouldn't just let me be. *I wanted to be alone with my mother.* I remember thinking that in the photo she looked worn out but still beautiful. Then the first captive who had asked for the magazine brought over a piece of candle and loaned me his reading glasses so that I could concentrate better. They all wanted to know what the article said. I was left with no other choice but to read the article aloud, although someone *else* wasn't happy about this and asked me to lower my voice so he could listen to the radio.

The article talked about the first rumors that my mother had a grandchild. Given the circumstances, I was pleased with her generous and straightforward response: "Come what may, I'll await them with open arms." And she fully kept her word. When a plane brought me back to freedom, she was the first person I recognized at the airport in Caracas, Venezuela. On my first day back in Colombia, when I went to pick up my son, who I hadn't seen in three years, she was the person who came with me. And she still accompanies us every day of our new life.

Thank you, dear mother of mine, for existing, and for being an example of kindness and dignity during moments of sheer pain.

3

The Day Before the
Kidnapping

FRIDAY, FEBRUARY 22, 2002,
BOGOTÁ, COLOMBIA

I arrived at campaign headquarters as fast as I could. It was around eleven in the morning, everyone was there, and the meeting had already started. There were about fifteen people in the room, among them Colombian senator Ingrid Betancourt, the presidential candidate for the liberal Green Party called Oxygen, which she'd founded in 1998, as well as her husband, the head of security, several press advisers, support personnel, and other campaign contributors.

The minute I walked in the room, Ingrid asked, "How did the television appearance go?"

"Fine," I said, "but it started a little late."

Then someone else in the room commented, "You're glowing." I let out a laugh and then, in a humble tone, said, "I still haven't managed getting used to speaking on television." After we all settled down, the meeting continued. My mind briefly rewound to the news show I had just been on, which dealt with the four million persons displaced by the armed conflict that had gripped Colombia for decades. A representative from each of the country's political parties debated the issue from its particular platform.

Suddenly I felt the tension in the room; everyone was worried about Ingrid's planned campaign stop the following day in San Vicente del Caguán, a remote municipality in Colombia's southern province of Caquetá, about an hour's flight from Bogotá.

Just a few days before, President Andrés Pastrana, having botched negotiations with the Revolutionary Armed Forces of Colombia (*Fuerzas Armadas Revolucionarias de Colombia*, acronymed FARC), had put an end to a twenty-four-square-mile demilitarized zone in southern Colombia that had been opened for the dialogue in 1998. The FARC, formed in 1964, is a Marxist-Leninist revolutionary guerrilla organization comprising approximately nine thousand to twelve thousand armed combatants and several thousand more supporters, mostly in rural areas of southern and eastern Colombia. Founded by Luis Morantes (alias Jacobo Arenas) and Pedro Antonio Marín (alias

Manuel Marulanda or Tirofijo), the FARC is organized along military lines and includes several urban fronts. It remains Colombia's oldest, largest, and best-equipped Marxist insurgency.

In November 1998, Pastrana began negotiations with the FARC and was able to meet with Marulanda. But after several breaks in the dialogue and mutual accusations that hindered further talks, the president announced on February 20, 2002, that he was ending the process based on his belief that the guerrillas didn't have true intentions of making peace. We now had to analyze the pros and cons of our candidate's traveling to the area under these new circumstances.

Everyone knew it was a dangerous journey because of the guerrilla presence, and there weren't many volunteers in the room that day willing to risk it. Then someone pointed out that this particular visit had been postponed more than once already and that the mayor of San Vicente, an Oxygen Party member, had personally asked if Ingrid could be there at a very delicate moment to back him publicly with her presence. The city's civilian population also concerned us since they lived so close to the FARC territory, and traveling there was a good opportunity to demonstrate our party's alternative to the country's current situation. It was a tense time in Colombia and the nation's concerns with security were at the forefront.

We discussed who could accompany the candidate, other than the two French journalists writing about her campaign, the press advisers, and the security team already set to go.

That's where we stood when Ingrid turned to me and asked, "Clara, would you come with me?" And I, without hesitation, replied, "But of course. What time do we leave?" I had hoped that my response would reestablish a feeling of confidence in the campaign and in the candidate; recapture some of that enthusiasm we had all felt just months before. As campaign director, it seemed that I should be sending a message to everyone by setting an example of loyalty and friendship. Especially given our current chaotic state: the week before, several of the campaign's directors, including the financial coordinator, the political coordinator, and a senator, resigned. And the campaign's spokesperson hadn't showed up for the meeting that day either.

So that's how I responded to Ingrid. Having stewed endlessly on it during those long years in captivity, I became convinced that my reaction that day could be categorized as a quixotic whim, if not flagrant stupidity. I was undoubtedly at the wrong place at the wrong time.

After the staff confirmed that we had to be at Bogotá's El Dorado International Airport at five o'clock the next morning, I went home for lunch. My studio apartment was only two blocks away from campaign headquarters. When I got there, I called my brother Carlos to tell him that I couldn't go to his country house the next day. He asked me why I had to go on the trip. I told him so that Ingrid didn't have to go alone and to show solidarity with San Vicente's mayor and its people. He wished me a good trip and a safe return and teased, "You know you're going to miss out on all the fun."

After lunch I went back to headquarters and spent the rest

of the afternoon going over work matters and other pending activities for the following week. It was only going to be an overnight excursion; our plan was to return to Bogotá Sunday afternoon. Around six in the evening, I left for the day. Just as I was walking in my front door, the intercom sounded; a friend was picking me up to go out to dinner. At the same time, the phone rang. It was the head of Colombia's national security. He wanted to inform me that he would be sending a fax that would explain in detail the potential dangers of our San Vicente del Caguán trip.

I called Ingrid on her cell phone. She and her husband were at a birthday party, and her husband, Juan Carlos Lecompte, answered her phone. When I told him about the fax, he put down the phone without a word and went to look for Ingrid, who took awhile getting on the line. She listened as I recounted what the security head had told me, then said, "Clara, if you don't want to go, stay. I'll travel anyway." Her reply felt a bit brusque, and I tried to calm her by repeating what I had been told. There was a long silence between us, which she eventually broke by saying, "I'll call you later."

By then my friend was at the door waiting to go. I asked him if we could order in dinner instead, explaining that I had to wake up very early the next day. Shortly after, Ingrid called again. I was surprised that she had left the party so soon. In a more conciliatory tone, she said, "Look, Clara, don't worry; nothing is going to happen to us. I'll send the driver early tomorrow, and we'll go to the airport together." I told her I'd still accompany her, but I did insist that she read all the information they had sent us by fax. After I hung up the phone, the food arrived with a delicious cold bottle of white wine. There was nothing more I could do at that moment but relax and enjoy the evening.

During captivity, I thought a lot about that night, going over each and every one of those moments again and again. Perhaps that's why it's still so fresh in my memory. The result of my intense reflection went like this: my mistake, if there was one, was made on that very day. Though it wouldn't have been easy, I should have been much more firm with Ingrid. I should have told her that I wasn't going to go with her, to see if she had the guts to go alone. Our story might have very well turned out differently if it had played itself out like this, and we wouldn't have had to suffer through this painful kidnapping chapter of our lives.

Obviously, none of this should have been done in an emotional manner, nor did it have to be a demonstration of absurd bravery. The fact was that we were two civilian women without any military training who expected to pass right in front of a rebel army that's had our country at a crossroads for nearly fifty years—though I do believe that while in captivity Ingrid and I ended up showing more discipline, courage, and determination than many of the other hostages, even those who were former military and police.

The truth is that our government never guaranteed us the necessary security for making that kind of trip. It would be offered to other presidential candidates later on, and it saved them from becoming hostages.

No, we never counted on such backing or the luck we had, for that matter. That's why I'm certain that the reason I'm still alive is a pure case of divine will. The first thing I do when I wake up, just before I'm conscious of taking my first breath, is thank God. I'm well aware of the miracle He worked for me.

My friend gave me a big hug and kiss good-bye that night. I'm not exaggerating when I say that it was the last kind gesture I would receive until the day I saw freedom again.

4

The Day

At four o'clock in the morning, my alarm went off. I took my time enjoying a long, hot shower, but even then I was still ready at four twenty. The driver was already waiting for me outside, and we headed over to pick up Ingrid. When we arrived at her duplex apartment in the mountains, she wasn't ready and made me come up. María, her longtime maid, immediately offered me a delicious glass of fresh tamarillo juice. In the company of Ingrid's golden Labrador, I waited, gazing out the living room window upon Bogotá. It was still dark, and you could look out over the entire capital with all its lights.

I snapped out of my daze when I suddenly heard someone shouting; it was Ingrid's husband calling the maid to bring him something upstairs. Shortly afterward, Ingrid came down. The sun was beginning to rise, and we were still on schedule. On our way to the airport, someone from our team called to confirm that San Vicente del Caguán's mayor and parish priest would be welcoming us that afternoon.

When we arrived at the terminal, the campaign's press chief and a load of camera people from Oxygen and the TV stations were already there ready to record our departure. The plane took off on time at six fifteen, and we flipped through the day's newspapers during most of the flight. The country's leading paper had published a story headlined "Ingrid's Campaign In Disarray; She's On Her Own."

Before we arrived in Florencia, the capital city of Caquetá, we had a layover in Neiva. There, in the VIP waiting room, we put together a press release stating that things weren't in disarray and that the candidate wasn't alone and planned on going forward at her typically vigorous pace. But despite our efforts at normalcy, the atmosphere still felt strained. It wasn't the best situation, to say the least, which led me to think about how her husband's loud tone that morning was coated with tension. And now this unduly downbeat newspaper story. I felt I should be supportive.

Despite having to wait a few hours in Neiva, we still arrived in Florencia before nine o'clock. We were greeted by friendly airport security personnel and taken to a special lounge where they informed us that two helicopters destined for San Vicente del Caguán were scheduled to leave shortly. Most likely they'd put us on one of them, we were told, but with only a few members from our delegation.

What followed was a never-ending stretch of hours. At around ten, we heard a loud noise in the air and watched as a squadron of police helicopters landed. Afterward, a large group of young, energetic men and women in their twenties arrived. They were a determined-looking bunch, moving briskly and carrying their equipment and police attire over their shoulders. The army officials waiting on the runway for them gave them orders to get into the helicopters and head to San Vicente del Caguán in preparation for the arrival of President Pastrana, who was scheduled to visit San Vicente del Caguán in order to demonstrate government support for the newly installed police force after the area's demilitarized zone status had been lifted. So the first flight out that day was filled with police.

Then a black Hercules military transport plane that had taken off from Bogotá landed. Out came a group of foreign journalists, also making a transfer, and who were apparently accredited to cover the presidential visit. Finally, around eleven, the presidential plane arrived and the president disembarked with Secretary General Juan Hernández, while the police force waited to pay its respects. On their way to the helicopters, the two men passed just a few feet in front of where we were standing on the runway. We followed Pastrana with our gaze, but he just kept walking. Without saying a word or so much as acknowledging us, he climbed into the helicopter and took off into the sky.

I must confess that I was stunned by his cold attitude, since he was always one to say a friendly hello. It seemed particularly strange that he would act this way toward Ingrid, given that their families were longtime friends; the two of them practically grew up together. Moreover, before he was elected president, she had been one of the star senators who'd traveled across the country seeking votes to contribute to his victory.

Suddenly, from one moment to the next, and without a clear explanation, we saw a procession of people boarding the remaining helicopters. Despite having told us when we arrived that we'd be boarding soon, they took off and left us behind. It turns out that for whatever reason, our campaign's chief of security couldn't get hold of the necessary accreditations to get us to San Vicente del Caguán by air as we had planned.

In retrospect, if the president's attitude had been different that day, the FARC guerrillas most likely wouldn't have kidnapped us. We would have traveled safely by helicopter and returned to Florencia and then to Bogotá as Pastrana, his delegation, and the international journalists had that very same night. Later that evening, fresh to captivity in the FARC camp, we would watch him on television. Oddly enough, our kidnapping wasn't reported until the following day. I don't know why it took so long, since our press chief lost contact with us at around two o'clock in the afternoon, allowing him plenty of time to announce our disappearance.

It's curious: there were few people I thought about as much in captivity as I did Pastrana. I suppose it came from that absurd notion that a country's president can fix all of its problems. When we were freed, he was one of the first former presidents to congratulate me on my bravery and to send me a letter, which I've stored for safekeeping. I'm convinced that he could have helped prevent our kidnapping or at least negotiated with our captors once we were held hostage. An attempt at our freedom should have come through an agreement or some negotiated solution—not through the military rescue operation that he ordered two days into our captivity, in which several of our army's soldiers were killed. But one must not forget that Pastrana was five months away from the end of his term. It seemed to me by that stage of his presidency, he was already on his way out, and perhaps that's why he overlooked his duties.

Something else about the president's trip to San Vicente del Caguán the same day as the Oxygen Party candidate's visit there has always struck me as strange. Was it merely a coincidence? His trip wasn't confirmed until the night before, and I would venture to say that perhaps he rushed ahead with his trip when he found out about ours. However, I don't have enough information to form any conclusions on this.

When we realized that the airport had been cleared out, we were left with no other choice than to travel the one hundred miles to San Vicente del Caguán by land. Florencia's Administrative Department of Security (DAS) agreed to set us up with a blue pickup truck but without any personnel to accompany us. So our group gathered in a small airport lounge to decide which of us would continue on. First the head of police security announced that he wouldn't be joining us, and the remaining bodyguards backed him. I don't know the reason for this decision, especially since his orders were to protect Ingrid throughout Colombian territory. Next a French journalist, her translator, and our press chief also announced that they were going to stay.

The entourage was reduced to five people: Ingrid, the driver, a French journalist, a camera assistant, and me. The captain of security helped us out by at least placing Ingrid Betancourt campaign posters and white flags on the vehicle; at one point he said to me, "Don't worry, madam. Tomorrow we'll be here to pick you up for your afternoon flight back to Bogotá."

That calmed me a bit. The truth was, up until that point, visits to rural, and potentially risky, areas of Colombia had always gone well for us. I remembered a similar trip on which I had accompanied Ingrid in 1997, while she was still in the Chamber of Representatives, the lower house of Colombia's congress. We took a small plane to Puerto Asís, a southern city that borders Ecuador's Putumayo region, to offer humanitarian aid, food, medical supplies, and clothing to the families who had taken to the streets to march together while they waited for their national government to resolve their demands. When we arrived, the airport had been sealed off by the army, and we barely had time to speak to the strikers, give them their supplies, and take a quick walk through the town before we had to return. But on the way back, the plane developed mechanical problems, forcing our pilot to make an emergency landing in a field near the Ibagué airport. Local firemen took us to the airport, and we flew back to Bogotá on a commercial flight.

In spite of the setbacks, I somehow expected this trip to San Vicente del Caguán to turn out as well as that trip to Puerto Asís. Because of this memory, the security captain's reassuring words were actually able to allay my fears a little.

Once the pickup truck was ready, we boarded. Ingrid went up front with the driver, while the French journalist, the cameraman, and I sat in the row behind them. We said our goodbyes to the bodyguards and the rest of the group, and were escorted by a Florencia police vehicle to the outskirts of the city. The road itself wasn't as bad as we expected and was practically empty, though every now and then we'd pass a taxi or someone on a moped.

We made our way along a beautiful stretch of savanna where the temperature was about eighty-five degrees in the shade. We passed an army checkpoint where they informed Ingrid that there hadn't been any recent combat in the area or on the road to San Vicente del Caguán. Nevertheless, the soldiers warned her that if she continued on, it would be at her own risk, and she'd be completely on her own. We agreed to stay on route. An hour into the trip, we stopped for fuel in the small town of Montañitas. Since we hadn't heard from our security team, we tried contacting them ourselves by cell phone, but with no success.

With a full tank of gas, we continued on a road that grew more solitary by the minute. The sky was filled with flocks of white birds as well as flocks of black ones—perhaps an omen for what waited just ahead. Next we came upon a series of bridges to cross. Over each one, I suffered in silence at the thought that they could very well be rigged with mines.

About thirty to forty minutes had passed since our last stop when we saw a stretch of road that went on for miles. From a distance, we could see trucks and buses parked on either side of the road blocking any traffic from passing. A young man wearing camouflage gear and carrying a rifle on his shoulder signaled us to stop. Our driver slowed down. Suddenly the lookout came running toward us. He approached the driver's side window and asked where we were headed. I noticed that on his belt he wore a sharp-edged machete, or *peinilla*.

We told him that they were waiting for us in San Vicente del Caguán and to please let us pass. He responded by telling us to wait; that he had to go ask one of his superiors. The young man was sweating and seemed visibly agitated. We watched him run toward the empty buses—there was nobody else in sight. A little while later, he was back.

"Follow me with your vehicle. Slowly," he ordered. He walked besides our truck and before we reached the buses, he instructed us to veer left. A pair of men who were dressed like peasants, but were actually guerrillas, appeared and motioned for us to head right this time, in order to pass between the buses. We were met with a strong smell of gasoline that seemed to be coming from one of the burnt-out vehicles, as if it were about to explode.

Once we passed the buses, we came to a clearing where a group of uniformed, armed men began surrounding our truck. They were very tense. Suddenly we heard a loud explosion that came from somewhere close by. It hit one of the men standing beside the truck, and blood started pouring down his face. The cameraman screamed, "Oh my God!" and we all sat there in shock.

Sounding desperate, one of the guerrillas shouted, "Fast, to a hospital!" They lifted the wounded man into the back of the truck and the young man with the rifle got in as well. He gave us directions on where to go, making us turn off the main road and onto a smaller one. All the while, the wounded man never stopped yelling from the pain. We hadn't been on the road ten minutes when we came upon several parked cars and a large group of armed, sweaty, nervous, nasty-looking men.

They signaled for us to stop. The wounded man was immediately unloaded and placed in a jeep that tore away at full speed. Then they turned their attention to us. The cameraman and the French journalist were asked to step out. At that moment, an intimidating man with gruff gestures—he must have been the *comandante*—arrived at the scene. They asked that Ingrid step out, and they put her into another truck facing the opposite direction.

At this point, I was alone in the truck. The comandante walked back to look at me. Worried, I asked him, "Where are you taking her?" He didn't answer and told me to get out. He put me in the same vehicle with Ingrid, but in the back part, where six other men, three on each side, sat in silence under a canvas covering. Two more men were holding on to the back-door from the outside of the truck. The minute I got in, it sped off onto a rough trail of undergrowth. It's completely possible that they knew we were going to be passing through that area; whatever the case, the men knew exactly what they were doing when they took Ingrid out of the vehicle. They were perfectly aware of who they were kidnapping.

The two men hanging onto the door began to hoot and holler as if they were having fun. Both were holding hand grenades, and I became frightened at the thought that one might get dropped and detonate, since the truck was jumping so much. I was in such anguish that I screamed to the driver, "Hey, you're not hauling potatoes back here!" I don't know if he heard me, but we did slow down a little. Soon after, we arrived at another spot, where we changed trucks again. This time an older and more relaxed comandante appeared and instructed us to sit with him in the front of another vehicle.

The other men stayed behind. We continued along a road that led to a small town called La Unión Pinilla. It was a calm and unusually quiet place: its inhabitants sat on rocking chairs on their porches. But there was complete silence as they all watched us go by. The comandante stopped the vehicle and made us go into a store with him. This was a good thing, since Ingrid and I both had to use the bathroom.

The owner approached and asked us if we wanted sodas. When we returned from using the bathroom, they made us go into a side room. The comandante instructed us to sit down and write a letter to our families informing them that we'd been kidnapped. I felt myself go pale, more so when he handed me a blank sheet of paper and then asked for my shoe size. It was precisely at that moment that I realized we were now captives. Up until then, I could still cling to the hope that they were going to free us. Like a large number of Colombia's inhabitants, I was very familiar with the tragedy and human drama surrounding kidnappings, but it's something that you hear about and never think can happen to you. Despite my awareness that there were people close to me who were at risk, never did I fathom that I could be a target.

Ingrid wrote a letter to her parents and her sister telling them what had happened. Then she passed the sheet of paper to me so I could read it and write a letter to my mother on the other side. I was barely capable of adding a short paragraph that read something like this:

My dearest mother,

I am confident that things happen in this life for a reason. I trust that being with Ingrid in the middle of

this outrageous conflict might somehow help stabilize our
everyday lives in Colombia. Trust in God at every moment.
I hope to be with you again soon,

Your beloved daughter

Afterward, without us knowing, the comandante must have faxed the letter to Ingrid's father's apartment.

They made us leave the store and get back into the truck. Again we sat alongside the comandante in the front, while a group of armed guerrillas occupied the cargo bed. It was already early evening by then, probably close to five o'clock. We left that town as if everything were completely normal; the townspeople in their rockers didn't bat an eyelash as they watched our vehicle pass by again. Once we reached a highway, the driver picked up speed. The mood inside the truck was tense. Perhaps that's why the comandante decided to put on some music. Ingrid and I remained silent. After a few long minutes passed, the only thing that the comandante had to say to us was that there was no solution to the situation we were in, and that the only thing we could do was to face up to the experience ahead of us.

A few hours later, under a dark nighttime sky, the driver veered off the main road. He drove for about a mile through a large field until we entered a grove that led us to the guerrilla camp. After we were told to get out of the truck, we were greeted by a female comandante who offered us her hand. I was surprised at how friendly she was and then by the strength of her grip: although she was only of medium height and had plenty of gray hair, I thought she was almost going to tear my arm off. Later on we found out that the comandante who had brought us there was named José Cebas, also known as *el Mocho César*. He'd headed the fifteen-person FARC squad that had kidnapped Ingrid and me, and he was also considered a confidant to the secretariat—the organization's seven-member ruling body. El Mocho César told us that we were now in her hands and that he'd return in two days. Her name was Mary Luz.

She showed us where we'd be sleeping that night. It was a place they referred to as "the hospital," but it was actually a huge shed, a type of barrack hut with a palm roof, dirt floor, and no walls. There were several sick men already in there, and we were given two cots in the corner, several empty mattresses away from the rest of them. They assigned us another woman guerrilla who was never to lose sight of us. We asked if we could go to the bathroom and were then directed to exit the hospital.

She called over another female comrade, and they made us walk about thirty paces until we reached a thicket where the ground was spotted with odd-looking holes. Due to the mud, the holes were filled with a yellowish liquid that made a dreadful impression on me. When it was my turn to go, I asked the guard if she could stand back a bit because my stomach was upset and I was embarrassed by the situation. But in the end, the change was so drastic that my body wasn't able to do a thing. It was all too much, with the mud, the yellow water, seeing all those ants and enormous leaves, many of them with thorns; all of it made me acutely aware of what was happening to us. When I got up again, we went back to the hospital.

On our short trip back, we were approached by comandante Mary Luz and two other women. She asked how we were and then began interrogating Ingrid on her political plans. A black cat approached us and perched beside the comandante, as if it were listening in on Ingrid's talk. We stood like this for a few minutes, and afterward they took us back to our sleeping quarters. I sat on the bed and stared at the dirt floor. The uniformed women with their long hair stood close by; some were huge, and I found them intimidating. I remained quiet; the thought of going to sleep in this place was strange. One of the women brought us two generous plates of white rice with a fried egg on top and a plantain. Though we hadn't eaten breakfast or lunch, it still seemed like a lot of food to me. She had only brought one spoon, so I asked her to bring one for me. For a moment, she just stood there looking at me and then went to bring us another one. It was strange to eat rice without a fork. We hardly touched our food.

It was after seven o'clock when the comandante arrived to take us somewhere else. The night sky was clear and well lit by the moon. We walked a few paces to another hut similar to the one we'd just left, though this one had long rectangular boards as makeshift benches. A television was on, and you could hear the sound of an electric generator in the background. They sat us down, and a little while later a group of armed but (luckily) relaxed-looking men walked in. We were going to watch the news, but since it was the weekend, it started later than usual, at eight. The reception was terrible, and though it was a color television, the image came through in black and white. There was no mention of us in the program's top stories. They only broadcast a quick segment about the president's trip to San Vicente del Caguán, saying that control over the city had already been regained. After that, the guerrillas turned off the television.

We were told to go back to the same hut, or *caleta,* where we'd been before. Along the way, I asked the comandante if we could stay outdoors and walk around a bit more around the caleta. She accepted our request, and we continued walking. We felt we had taken a step forward, in more ways than one, and discussed what we had heard on the news. We worried about whether the other comandante, el Mocho César, had faxed our letter to our families already, and if it had arrived, if they had even read it yet. Not knowing what was happening back home had our stomachs in knots.

Soon enough they informed us that it was time to go to bed. It was around nine or ten at night at most. When we got back to the caleta, we noticed that there weren't any sheets, just a board with a very thin mattress. They set up a mosquito net over the two beds, and we decided to sleep together in one of them. I wouldn't dare move an inch, I was so affected by it all: the darkness, those sick men with weapons at their sides, so close by.

A guard with a lantern would pass by every so often to check up on us. Though there was complete silence all around us, give or take a few of your typical night sounds, I still couldn't sleep. Then it started to rain, and I finally was able to relax a bit and close my eyes. I was awoken by the sound of helicopters and asked God to let it keep raining so that the army would have trouble reaching our camp. I kept thinking about the tragic death of Diana Turbay, a thirty-seven-year-old journalist and daughter of former Colombian president Julio César Turbay Ayala. She was kidnapped by narcotraffickers on January 25, 1991. After four months of captivity, Turbay died in a failed rescue attempt during a shoot-out between the police and the drug smugglers working for Colombian cocaine kingpin Pablo Escobar. My legs trembled with fright.

Out of nowhere, the comandante arrived, looking nervous, and she told us to get out of bed. This was an easy task, given that we had slept with our clothes on. We left the camp and hiked for about thirty minutes in the middle of dense jungle. Though it had stopped raining, everything was wet, and my sneakers got soaked. We walked in a straight formation, one in front of the other; it was pitch black, and you couldn't see where you were stepping. We could barely detect the other armed guerrillas around us; they moved in such a stealth manner. You could only hear the comandante's voice. Every once in a while, she made us stop in the middle of nowhere. We stood perfectly still in that jungle, even as the mosquitoes swarmed around us. It was exhausting just standing there. A little while later, we resumed our march until we reached a place that turned out to be the one we'd first left.

They made us get underneath our mosquito net once again. It was cold, and I was sweating, and I tried to figure out what time it was, calculating that it had to be close to one or two o'clock in the morning. This time I fell asleep right away from utter exhaustion. It was too much for just one day.

5

The Day After

It was the crack of dawn, and the first thing I remember was the strong smell of gasoline. Somewhere close by, a radio was announcing that we'd been kidnapped. It was cloudy and drizzling, and I got out of bed with a deep feeling of worry in my gut. I asked the guard if I could use the bathroom, and she brought me to the same area as the night before. But this time you could actually see the scenery: an immense jungle and, in the distance, a vast plain. I had a feeling that we had to be close to the little town they'd brought us to, La Unión Pinilla. When we got back to the caleta, I was immediately made dizzy again by the gasoline smell, and I asked if I could stay outside.

It was still dark out, though it had stopped raining, and they pointed to some boards I should sit down on right outside from where we slept. I'd been sitting there alone for a while before a young guerrilla came over to talk to me. I was surprised to see that he didn't have a rifle on him and that he was walking around in only a green T-shirt and camouflage pants. He was clean shaven, fair skinned, and appeared very relaxed. He asked me how I was doing. "Fine," I told him tersely. He was curious to know if I had felt scared the night before.

"Of course," I said. "It was the first time in my life my legs had trembled like that from fear. Then I was nearly paralyzed by the sound of the helicopters above." He let out a laugh, which surprised me, and added, "That was nothing."

Some time had passed, when another young female guerrilla approached me to ask if I wanted something to drink. As if I were back in the city, I responded that I'd like some orange juice. A little while later, she came back with two fresh-squeezed glasses of mandarin juice and indicated that one was for me and the other for my friend. I drank it down, and later on I'd remember that moment, particularly the fruit's color, as one of my most special moments during captivity. In that moment, naïve me could not imagine what was coming next—that I'd have to wait several years to smell the scent of a fruit juice again. Even today, now that I'm free, each time I drink a glass of orange juice at breakfast, I relish it as one of the most pleasurable delicacies that one can have. And I thank God.

It was around seven thirty when Ingrid emerged from our caleta. She appeared incredibly thin and walked over to me with a look of shock on her face and said hello. I asked her how she was doing. Seeming as if she didn't want to talk, she replied that she had cried all night. I told her that she must have cried only on the inside because I hadn't heard a peep out of her. But in reality, her lack of sleep showed on her face. She sat down next to me, and I offered her the juice and told her about what I had heard on the news. According to the radio program, the news about our kidnapping had even been reported in the *Washington Post*. We both remained quiet afterward. It was just so hard to grasp what was happening to us.

We went to the bathroom and on the way back asked the guard if we could walk around the camp to familiarize ourselves a bit with where we were. In one of the other huts, we spotted a hanging woven work. It looked like a cord of string supporting a parachute's meshlike fabric, though it was probably a fishing net. Further along this path, we saw portable chairs with dental instruments. Behind those there was a kind of pantry—what they called their post exchange—with potatoes, plantains, and vegetables. To the side of it stood a pair of gas burners and a barrel filled with water. We kept walking and arrived at comandante Mary Luz's barrack hut. You could tell that someone of authority lived there, because it had a bedroom-looking setup toward the back and even a refrigerator in the anteroom. Though it still had dirt floors like ours, it was the best place we had seen since our arrival. We were also taken aback when we spotted one of the female guerrillas painting her toenails. I was dumbfounded: the last thing I expected to see that first morning, was our tough female captors acting as if they were in a beauty salon.

Inside the mood was calm. Nothing like what we had experienced the night before. We asked if we could wash ourselves, and they told us we would have to wait a few hours until the bathing pool was free. Ingrid took advantage of the situation to ask for a mat to do her exercises on, and I requested a chess set.

When we got back to our quarters after our short walk, they had left us a very dark, almost black, cup of hot chocolate. I tried it and thought how bitter and thick it tasted; not like a real hot chocolate with hot, foamy milk. I sat inside our hut and looked up at the ceiling. The day was grey, and there was hardly any light, so I lay down and tried to rest a bit. I felt incapable of saying anything, since I could barely understand what was happening.

Soon they told us to get ready for our baths, yet they hadn't given us anything to bathe with. They eventually brought us towels and led us to a large cement sink from which we filled tins they'd given us with water. Not knowing where to leave our clothing, I decided to hang mine from a branch. To avoid getting mud on us, we undressed with haste while standing on top of the wooden boards. The water was ice cold, and there was hardly any soap. I rinsed off and got dressed within seconds. But the shower made me feel like a new person despite it being so quick. Afterward, we went back to our hut, where I had a brush in my purse, and I took my time grooming myself. Sometime past noon, they offered us a lunch that consisted of cold, hard pieces of meat on a skewer with a pair of tomatoes.

We remained in our quarters that whole afternoon without doing anything in particular. When it began to get dark out, they brought us a bag with bread and a beverage called *agua de panela*, which consists of water sweetened with a piece of *panela*, a nutrient extracted from sugarcane. It was overly sweet but another highlight after the mandarin juice. Later on I'd learn that in the jungle, they make their drinks highly concentrated and very sweet for energy purposes.

Just before eight o'clock, they took us to watch the news. The headlines confirmed that we'd been kidnapped by the Fifteenth Front of the FARC, commanded by Joaquín Gómez (real name: Milton de Jesús Toncel Redondo). Upon hearing the news, about twenty of the guerrillas that were in the room began to shout and jump around. I was stunned at how happy they were for having kidnapped us.

When the news was over, they took us back to our quarters. I remained mute, still terribly affected at having seen our kidnapping portrayed as a fait accompli on television and by the thought of the guerrillas' utter joy. I lay down on my bed repeating to myself: "My God, I'm a hostage, I'm really a hostage!" The tears poured down my face. I was exhausted. The night was pitch black. With a pain in my soul, I closed my eyes and trusted in God until I was overcome with sleep.

Today, when I look back on that day and try to remember what thoughts passed through our heads, I can't. Nor do I remember having an important conversation with Ingrid, either. The cruel reality into which we'd been plunged was, without a doubt, beyond our capacity of understanding.

6

The Jungle

Having always lived in the city, I suffered a great deal from being kept in such a rural environment, constantly surrounded by weeds, practically engulfed in them. It's hard to imagine that as a little girl I had loved everything having to do with nature and conserving the environment. But it's one thing to love nature and another to feel yourself being devoured by her. That jungle, as we would soon discover during our attempts at escaping, became our jail cell, rendering every effort to flee futile.

You're always in the shade in the jungle; direct sunlight doesn't get through. And when it does, it arrives filtered through the thick foliage of gigantic trees that can stand as tall as six or seven stories. In fact, guerrillas always choose campgrounds located in the densest parts of the jungle so that they can avoid being spotted by army planes. Due to the lack of sunlight, you become pale and develop problems with your eyesight over time. The jungle has its color; it's a green of a thousand tones. It also has its own scent, of vegetation and humidity, which ends up impregnating your own skin.

It's an unhealthy environment with an asphyxiating climate. The days are so hot and muggy that any type of physical activity, like the long treks we were subjected to, felt even harder to do. At night, the temperature drops drastically at around three o'clock. Since they had taken our watches, and the cold was so intense at that hour, I calculated the time starting from then.

Life in the jungle has a set routine, imposed by all the difficulties and determining factors that this hostile environment can have on its human inhabitants. All our days were exactly the same. We woke up at dawn and headed to the *chonto,* an excavated hole in the ground about three feet deep and one and one-half feet in diameter that served as a latrine. That's where we took care of our bodily needs, covering it up with dirt each time. Afterward, we'd wash up however we could, and at around six o'clock, they'd bring us a hot black coffee (*tinto*) sweetened with panela. Upon finishing, we'd pack it all up again and hit the road.

During that first phase of our kidnapping, the FARC guerrillas kept us in constant movement—rarely did we spend time in one place—going deeper and deeper into the jungle in order to avoid the army following our trail, trying to save us. We were obligated to change location practically every day, and we would trek by foot for excruciating distances. When we went by motorboat, we had to cover our heads in plastic and keep them lowered so that nobody would recognize us. It was a nomadic life where we always had to be ready to flee. Our equipment was always packed, for at any moment they could tell us we had to keep going.

On those long walks, each one of us had to, as they say, carry their home on their back. In addition to your personal belongings, you lugged a canvas hammock, mosquito net, and an army tent that we used as a roof when it rained. Sometimes we slept on the ground or over palm tree leaves, like animals.

It happened once that we had to travel by mule, since the trail was so long and rough. Supposedly the guerrillas had only one saddle, so they asked me if I knew how to ride bareback. I told them I didn't but that I'd try, and that's how I rode during the roughly eight-hour journey. When I got off the animal, I collapsed to the ground. I was as tired and smelly as the mule itself, with whom I also had to share the little water that was left. That trip was debilitating but strangely pleasant, especially during sunset when we had to go up a mountain and could make out the plain below. The scenery was spectacular. The crystal clear sky and the sun filled me with incredible energy despite the pain that my legs were causing me; they were practically raw and peeling from all the friction during the ride.

Later on I found out that there *was* another saddle; they

didn't give it to me for fear that I'd escape. And I have to admit that the thought crossed my mind while I was atop that animal's back. I began to think that the trail we were taking had to lead to somewhere. But I convinced myself that I'd better not take the chance: I was surrounded by at least a dozen armed guerrillas on foot.

Around that time, the two comandantes who had greeted us, el Mocho César and Mary Luz, decided to stay behind. We never saw either of them again. Much later, we would learn that in October of that year, el Mocho had been shot and killed by the army in an attempt to rescue us, while Mary Luz was captured somewhere close to San Vicente del Caguán a few years later.

We were eventually assigned new comandantes and a different squad to keep an eye on us. That's when our real pilgrimage through the jungle began. Each day we walked until nightfall and stopped when it was time to fix our camp for the night. A pair of guerrillas would clear a small area within the weeds, trim some branches and palm leaves to build a kind of hut, and then hammer in stakes on which to hang their jackets and bags. On occasion, there wasn't enough time to build that simple structure, and we just slept in our hammocks out in the open, with a mosquito net and the tent's canvas over us. I almost preferred sleeping on the ground, even if it was on a bunch of palm leaves. The hammock was very narrow and uncomfortable, but there were times that the ground was wet or full of insects and animal life. Sleeping on a cushion on top of wooden boards, as we did at our original quarters, was a complete luxury in comparison.

Once we'd prepared our place to sleep, I'd wash myself—sometimes in a river, if I could. But the majority of the times, I cleansed myself *totumadas* style, as we say in Colombia: using the hollow shell of the calabash fruit (*totuma*) as a container for water. In my case, I settled for the metallic dishware I used for food. I also took advantage of this time to wash the green army camouflage I was given to wear that was always drenched in sweat by the end of the day. I'd throw on the change of clothes that I had and lay the other set out to dry. But there'd be those mornings when my gear was still damp, and that's how I had to wear it. After I finished the wash, I ate and fell right to sleep until dawn the next day.

It was a forced immersion into the most rugged and uninviting of environments. The equatorial jungle is dense, hot, humid, and oppressive. Its dim floors are a moist clay layer, with colors that run the gamut from yellow to brown. It's the kingdom of mud—*el chuquio*, as they refer to it there.

It is home to all types of birds, mammals, reptiles, and amphibians. There are animals and insects of all colors, shapes, and sizes: from small spiders to enormous ones; brown-colored scorpions; black and reddish ones; ants of every size, from the tiny ones to those creepy crawlers capable of devouring you alive; flying cockroaches; mosquitoes; daddy longlegs; bees; wasps; bumblebees—evidently, plenty of creatures to protect yourself from at all times.

I have to confess that I found it all unnerving. I was too much of a city dweller, and it showed. Each day I would try to wake up with a better attitude, raising my arms to the sky and thanking God for being alive and for the all the beautiful things you could find in that place, in spite of it all. But when we had to keep walking in the middle of that terribly dense jungle, along those inhospitable trails, the sweat dripping from my forehead would often mix with the tears running from my eyes. I felt as if I had reached the very end of the world and I was practically on my own.

I still find it hard to understand how the inhabitants of those isolated areas survive: without any roadways other than rivers, without boats, without food or medical supplies, without clothing or appropriate footwear, without any type of information, without access to a television or radio, not even a newspaper. Nor is there electricity or appropriate combustible supplies for cooking food, or resources for constructing homes, except ones made out of wood and damp palm leaves. And those materials are continually prey for termites and weevils.

But that impenetrable jungle was our setting, and we had to survive in it, despite the difficulties and everything it lacked.

It would be impossible to forget the first time I saw a jaguar up close. Even though it was already dead, it made a huge impression on me. During our first weeks of captivity, the comandante who was formerly in charge of us would come up with ways to remind us that we were in the middle of a jungle. One morning he showed up at the camp with the bloody head of a jaguar. From the size of it, you could tell that it belonged to a large animal. Afterward, we saw him wearing a necklace from which hung the fangs that he just extracted from the beast.

It's true that after a few months, I got more used to living in that kind of environment, where you're always on the look-out for animals. One evening, when it was beginning to get dark, I was finishing up a bath in the river—at this early stage of the kidnapping, they still allowed me to wade or swim in it—when all of a sudden I heard a loud scream followed by the sound of struggling guerrillas' voices. I wondered what could have happened to create such a ruckus.

That's when I saw a group of guerrillas dragging a huge yellow and brown-streaked snake that had to be at least twenty feet long and twenty inches around. They struggled with the snake, though there were several of them carrying it. Then they hacked it to pieces as if it were the trunk of a tree. I couldn't help but think that its leathery skin would make for more than just one exquisite purse. The comandante, in his usual forceful tone, told me that I should stop swimming in the river.

"For that breed of snake, you're not even a mouthful," he said. Mockingly, I answered back, "Right, because if it ate someone nice and plump like you, it would feel satiated, correct?" Apparently he didn't like my tone; just as I expected, a few days later the comandante took away my right to bathe in the river.

It got to the point where other types of snakes, the ones that were about three feet long and could find their way into our barrack hut, no longer made such an impression on me. But in any case, I was instantly startled whenever someone screamed that he or she had seen one, which happened at least once a month and whenever it rained.

There were also smaller creatures to give us a good scare, as happened one morning when I was putting on my boots. I was lucky that my parents had taught me that whenever you're in a hot climate, be sure to shake out your clothing before putting it on. Especially your shoes, since spiders and scorpions love to crawl inside them. Such lessons from childhood always stuck with me, and I still abide by them. And that's what I did one morning before sticking my foot into my boot. I turned it over and was horrified when an eight-inch brown-colored tarantula fell out. I can still remember its pincers. I threw the boot on the floor and froze until it scurried away. It was a close call, especially since you couldn't even rely on getting an aspirin in that place to ease the pain, much less intravenous fluids.

The ants were an entirely different case. One night when we had already joined up with another hostage group and were retiring for the night, I heard a crackling sound on the ground after climbing into my hammock. I got down and screamed, "Oh my God!" when I realized that the ground was filled with gigantic ants over an inch long. Everywhere I moved, there they were. I was overwhelmed: I didn't have my lantern or even my lighter on me and began to scream like a crazy person. But not one of the other hostages said or did a thing, for possible fear that the guerrillas might think it was an uprising. Or that's what they told me the next day. My gut told me that these people were so exhausted that they no longer had the reflexes to care. I kept screaming until the guard finally came over to me, with a lantern and a rifle on his shoulder, to say in a tone of reproach, "Clara, calm down already, the ants will go away! Move over and calm yourself!"

But my tent was already near a precipice, and I was less than fifteen feet away from the river, and because it was so dark, I didn't know where to head. I asked for water to drown them, but there wasn't any. I told the guard to at least offer me some light to find my defense tools in my bag: talcum powder to throw on the floor and toothpaste to apply onto the hammock's cord. At least with the powder, they dispersed somewhat. Since I ended up pouring the entire container over them, the ants probably even coughed a bit. When the lantern was on, I could see them: they were enormous, and I was barefoot! That night I wouldn't even lie down in the hammock again for fear they'd climb up on it. The next morning, I saw how they left the clothes I had hanging inside the tent full of holes. I was left with no choice but to throw them away and remain with what I had on. And I had to repair the tent. I named them the creepy crawlers. They'd attack again, but I already had had an experience that taught me not to succumb.

It's curious: yesterday I brought my son, Emmanuel, to

a children's musical where the protagonists had to travel through an enchanted forest and some foul waters. I found it incredible how everything that appeared to be fantasy and a game was completely a reality in the jungle. And that's exactly where Emmanuel and I came from: a dark and inhospitable jungle.

7

Night

As hostages in the jungle, nighttime didn't only represent the period of the day when clarity was absent, it also was when our feelings of despondency, fear, confusion, and melancholy rose to their highest pitch. It's the portion of the day when you have to face yourself, feel the exhaustion and the solitude, along with an entanglement of other emotions and thoughts that begin to seethe inside of you.

Nightfall in the jungle begins sometime after six thirty and consists of several phases. The first is the noise phase, when the cicadas, crickets, fireflies, frogs, and countless other animals set off a commotion that sounds like rush hour traffic. At around seven o'clock, the racket begins to subside, and darkness sets in. It becomes so thick that it's impossible to make out the fingers on your hand right in front of you. Eight o'clock to two o'clock brings the silent phase, and from three until dawn, the cold phase.

Each one of those nights, one after the other for six years of captivity, felt like an eternity that would add up to thousands of hours spent living with fear, loneliness, confusion, and sadness. It was indescribable and made worse by the fact that the majority of the time was spent in candlelight, being wary of the animals, a possible military attack, the rain, or the wind. Or it was simply the existential angst each one of us carried inside.

Nights when the moon was visible were especially harrowing. We practically slept out in the open, and everyone knows that the moon can generate very intense emotions and exacerbate feelings that can sometimes border on delirium. About a month after being kidnapped, I had one of those nights. My nerves were on edge: Ingrid and I had planned to escape the following night, and I seriously feared for our lives. So I spent the night staring at the moon, thinking to myself, "This is insane, may the Lord protect us."

During my pregnancy, I lived another similar night. I was close to six months and filled with such terrible anxiety that I wanted to tear my soul out. I walked out of those precarious accommodations where they were keeping me and spent the entire night sitting on a chair and staring at the sky. Over time I became more practical and tried staying put in my hammock during the nights I couldn't sleep; that way, at least I kept myself warm.

What a difference in comparison to the nights I now spend in freedom! It's surprising when people ask me if I have trouble sleeping. Why should there be a problem? All is happiness when you're free. In captivity, the night hours languished with an accumulated weight that grew harder to bear as the days went on.

8

The Guerrillas

Even before I was kidnapped, I kept track of news about the FARC like almost every other Colombian. Most of the time, the media portray the guerrillas as harmful and dangerous; they are condemned for all the barbarities they've carried out and for their ties to drug trafficking.

Despite all the headlines that the Revolutionary Armed Forces of Colombia make, I rarely read about their ideological struggles, except for the few articles written by journalists who became interested in their quintessential leaders: Manuel Marulanda, in charge of the FARC's military command; and Jacobo Arenas, in charge of its ideological direction.

Marulanda, who died of natural causes on March 26, 2008, at the age of seventy-eight, was criticized for trying to solve the country's problems by turning to violence, extortion, kidnapping, and drug trafficking, in a conflict that has lasted decades and claimed thousands of lives. As for Arenas, he considered himself a kind of successor to the Argentina-born revolutionary Ernesto Che Guevara, a man he admired, and instructed the FARC guerrillas in the Marxist-Leninist doctrine. Morantes-Jaimes/Arenas died of cancer in 1990.

I'd also read a few books about the rebel group's peace attempts in the 1980s and the rapprochements they reached with various administrations during the rare occasions that they could all sit together at the negotiating table. But the last unsuccessful attempt at negotiating a peace settlement between Colombia's government and the FARC, which fell apart in 2002, I was able to follow up close.

I must admit that from the very first moment, and almost until the end, I was cautious around the guerrillas, and I can't say that they ever inspired my sympathy. And I sense that the feelings were mutual, given my independent personality, my education, and my love for my country, my family, and those close to me.

But in any case, the contact we had with them was minimal. Everything was done through middle management and by the guards who were mere common-folk guerrillas. They came from humble, indigenous origins in the countryside, and usually from the southern municipalities. For the most part, they were there to watch over us, feed us, and attend to our basic needs. Rarely did they say a word to us. The majority were young, dynamic, illiterate people, ranging from eighteen to thirty-five years old, who had military and disciplinary training but lacked general knowledge of things having to do with their country, the world, and civilization.

They're also people with weak family ties who don't feel like they're part of the country or society as a whole. Some, in fact, were younger than eighteen. It was painful to see armed girls and boys, with rifles resting on their shoulders, chopping wood, carrying heavy loads, and guarding over us, while receiving minimal medical attention, one scant meal a day, and, on occasion, some clothing and toiletries. The only thing they were able to receive is what they themselves refer to as a *fariana* (relating to the FARC) education, with the level of indoctrination that it implies.

For that reason, they're all taught to think that their only possible existence and future reside with the FARC, especially when they join young and become adults among the guerrillas. They have passable intelligence and, more importantly, the acumen necessary to survive in that kind of environment. And, without a doubt, they also have plenty of what's known in Colombia as *malicia indígena,* or "innate cunning." This partly explains all their leaders' failures during various attempts at peace processes; they're just never capable of reaching a level of confidence with the Colombian government to allow them to advance with the negotiations.

I've been asked on several occasions if I had a chance to

have any serious talks with members of the FARC's secretariat* or with Manuel Marulanda himself. The answer is no. There were few words between us, since I rarely saw them during my captivity, and when I did, we were never able to establish a true exchange of ideas. Marulanda never came to see us in any of the locations where they held us captive, nor were we told that he had any interest in speaking with us.

We received word from him only once. That was during our first year as hostages, when el Mocho César brought us a note from him in which he offered his greetings. He said he hoped, despite the circumstances, that we were well and asked us to prepare a short message that would be videotaped and sent to our families and the press.

Those were the first "proof-of-life" recordings that the FARC made us do, and they were filmed in May 2002 while we were being held in the deepest parts of Colombia's southern jungles. Later on we found out that they were transmitted in July. That's how my family finally learned that I was still alive. Once we were set free, I discovered that Ingrid's family hadn't for-

---

* After the death of Marulanda, who served as top leader for more than forty years, Guillermo León Sánchez Vargas, aka Alfonso Cano, became the guerrillas' commander in chief. The secretariat suffered another loss on March 1, 2008, when another important member, Luis Edgar Devia Silva, aka Raúl Reyes, was killed during an aerial attack by the Colombian army in Ecuadorian territory. Reyes was replaced by Joaquín Gómez, in charge of the Southern Bloc. As of this writing, the other members of the secretariat are: Rodrigo Londoño Echeverri, aka Timoleón Jiménez; Jorge Briceño Suárez, aka Mono Jojoy; Luciano Marín Arango, aka Iván Márquez; Wilson Valderrama, aka Mauricio or El Médico; and Jorge Torres Victoria, aka Catatumbo.

warded the note I had written with her on the day we were kidnapped until months later. It seems they had an excessive need to maintain the spotlight despite the right my family had to that information. It was cruel on their part, withholding those words intended for my family, which would have been appreciated during their moments of anguish.

One year later, in May 2003, Comandante Joaquín Gómez came to gather more proof-of-life evidence from us, which I wasn't opposed to. I considered it an opportunity to send a message to my family—perhaps the last, as it would turn out to be. This was right after a Colombian army hostage-rescue attempt had cost the lives of the province of Antioquia's governor, Guillermo Gaviria Correa, his peace adviser, Gilberto Echeverri Mejía, and eight army soldiers. (Several survivors of the clash insist that the guerrillas shot the hostages to death in accordance with FARC law.) The tragedy incited such a huge uproar from the general public and the families of the other hostages in opposition to these types of military operations that it compelled the administration of President Álvaro Uribe to change its strategy.

I'd had a feeling that the army was very close, and I feared that we could be the next persons on their list for a military operation. This had us constantly on watch and in permanent angst. A few weeks after I was freed in 2008, a government minister confirmed that the army had discovered our location during that time and was able to place soldiers just a few hours away from where we were being held.

As I watched Gómez get out of his motorboat, I asked a female guerrilla, who had brought us our food, who he was and where he was from. She confirmed that it was Joaquín and that he was born in La Guajira, a province in northern Colombia that borders Venezuela. I imagined a man with good manners, typical of Colombia's coastal people. As he approached my quarters, a foul smell came my way, and I thought, "Look at that: these men also suffer from stomachaches and the runs when facing difficult situations." I remembered Gabriel García Márquez's book *The General in His Labyrinth*, in which he made a reference to the liberator's stomach troubles.

Joaquín was accompanied by a man named Martín Corea and a guerrilla leader named Comandante Fabián Ramírez, who introduced himself. I had planned to greet Joaquín amicably and said, "How's it going, Joaquín? You doing well?" His reply, to everyone's surprise, was equally friendly: "Hi, Clarita." Then he greeted Ingrid and walked out. Fabián and Martín Corea told me to wait there, which I did. When Fabián came back, he surprised me by asking about my family.

A little while later, Joaquín came back to talk with Ingrid and me. I don't know what possessed me to ask him about the recent massacre in Bojayá, in which hundreds of civilians seeking refuge in a church from the violent encounters between the guerrillas and the paramilitaries died when a FARC bomb exploded nearby. I immediately regretted having done so. My question put him in such a bad mood that when, later on, I had the nerve to ask him to free us, he responded with a flat-out *"No."* There was no expression on his face when he spoke his answer. The dryness of his tone so affected me that I retired back to my hut. I don't remember what excuse I used, but I remember I cried inconsolably, like a little girl, wetting my T-shirt. Soon after, Joaquín came to say good-bye, and I insisted, "Doesn't keeping us as hostages weigh on you somewhat?" He didn't bother to answer me and left.

A week later, he returned with a camera. I went first for what would be one of the most complicated scenarios of my life. Standing in front of me was the cameraman—Fabián Ramírez—and it turns out he wasn't bad. Ingrid was on one side of me, while Joaquín stood farther back. Behind him stood the seventeen members of the guerrilla squad that guarded us, plus others who had come for a visit. Armed and silent, they all watched closely. When I was about to start talking, Joaquín stood up, adjusted his revolvers, and put on a more serious face. Being that he was very thin, a bit shorter than me, and with a uniform that was too big on him, the whole scene seemed almost comical.

First, I thanked God, like I usually do. Then I don't know where I got the strength to talk for ten minutes straight about the situation we were in. I imagine my motivation came from just thinking about my mother and my family; above all, I wanted to send them a message that I can summarize like this: "I love you, and I will keep loving you, and what I want most is to be with you." It was true that at the start of each day, my first thoughts were always with my mother; I remembered all of her important lessons and those beautiful moments we shared together, and that's what gave me the fortitude to survive in the jungle.

Weeks later, in mid-2003, we were transferred to another front. Jorge Briceño Suárez, aka Mono Jojoy, an important member of the FARC's secretariat, was in charge. On the way, we were met by his right-hand man, the comandante Martín Sombra (born Hely Mejía Mendoza). I remember him particularly well because he blindfolded us with handkerchiefs when we were transported by truck from one location to the next. Sombra is your prototypical fired-up guerrilla—cautious, suspicious, and shrewd—who belonged to the old guard in the mountainous region of Marquetalia, where the peasant rebels first took up weapons in 1964. He was nicknamed "the warden" because he was merciless with his captives. There was no doubt that Mono Jojoy had the utmost confidence in Sombra; he could count on his top-notch guerrilla experience to be in charge of such an enormous group of hostages, comprised of twenty-eight military soldiers and police, three Americans, and dozens of civilians, among them former congressmen, governors, and four women, including me.

On one occasion, Sombra prepared for Mono Jojoy to visit our camp. But from what I recall, he passed right through and didn't say a word to any of the hostages. Just a few months before, we had run into him, and he greeted us quickly and congratulated me for my proof-of-life recording by saying, "Clara, you're great on camera." I remained quiet, not expecting to hear this sort of comment from him. After what had happened with Joaquín Gómez, I didn't have it in me again to ask that he free us.

9

A Sense of Decency

The word *pudor,* in Spanish, means an honorable sense of
shame. This was my chosen disposition during captivity. In
all honesty, I understood the word to mean decency, modesty,
and reserve. To be reasonable and just. It seemed that from
the very first moment I realized I was a captive, I understood
it as the best way to behave. When did God shed light on this
for me? It also came naturally to me, since I was educated to
behave in this manner.

I first adopted this attitude in the jungle when facing myself, but also when facing my friend Ingrid, the one I decided
to accompany, as well as my country, its government, its sover-
eign states, and my fellow hostages.

I speak of honesty because there wasn't anyone, if given
the chance, with whom I didn't voice my thoughts or my

hopes of being freed. This I always did with the utmost respect for their opinions; although I must admit there were times I didn't agree with them, felt bothered by them, or found them simply hilarious.

I always acted with reserve in the face of sorrow, new information, or if I had differences with others. Before I reacted, I always looked for spaces to try to digest, ponder, and understand the facts I was being dealt.

Living with the other hostages in these situations of extreme uncertainty—where you live in perpetual fear that a face-off between the army and the guerrillas could erupt and kill you at any second—was extremely hard to handle. But it was unavoidable, and it caused tensions between us. It would be pointless for me to go into detail, as well as hard for me to revisit each and every incident. Nor is it my place to judge the other prisoners' attitudes, especially today, when they still remain incomprehensible to me. I don't want even to try to speculate on the thoughts in their heads or their hearts, for I'd run the risk of getting it wrong. I prefer to limit myself to saying that the relationships among the hostages were extremely tense during most of our captivity. Of course, I, like everyone else, made mistakes and was driven mad more than once despite my efforts at remaining calm.

But I believe that thanks to this attitude that I've synthesized in the word *pudor*, I was able to gain a level of credibility and respect that over time helped me in my daily chore to survive and to avoid added problems in captivity. My conscious is clear because of this, and it's allowed space for reconciliation.

10

Friendship

At an early age, I was taught the value of friendship, and it still remains an essential factor in my life. First, I want to pay tribute to the person who was perhaps my closest friend: my father. We shared many special moments together that I will always take with me in spirit. Throughout my childhood, he showed me what friendship was by always being a dedicated friend to his friends. My father died at the age of seventy-four, and on the day of his burial, in 2001, many of them spoke to me about the void his passing had left. He was the kind of person who was generous with his time and his advice; a happy man with a respectful and selfless demeanor.

He made me understand that besides being my father, he was, and would always be, my friend. He spoiled me; he spent what's referred to as quality time with me. My education was always of great concern to him. Because I was the youngest of five children and the only daughter, he was intent that I learn how to get by on my own. And he prepared me for this. He made sure never to favor me over the others because he wanted me to learn to value myself first. This was the spirit of his education, and he was behind my every step until I graduated from college. When I got my first job working part-time in a law office, I knew he was proud. During college, I'd save up my money every year so I could travel somewhere, and my parents would match that sum with their own money. This way I was able to work during the year and spend my vacations in different places around the world.

Friendship has always signified a way of getting close to others without any ulterior motives and expecting nothing in return. There is also something to learn about the value of giving oneself to others, as well as its limits. My father would say, "Clara Lety"—my middle name is Leticia, and that's what my parents liked to call me—"a good friend even accompanies their friends to the cemetery, but they don't bury themselves with them."

Perhaps that was also his way of preparing me for when he was gone: a reminder to not let myself drown in sorrow and pain and to keep going. And certainly, when that moment arrived, it was very hard for me to deal with. When we were kidnapped, it had been barely a year after his death, and I was still in mourning. But in his absence, I was finally able to reflect on all his teachings. They were clearer in my memory than ever before, and with them I could take on the harrowing test of captivity in the jungle.

When it became clear that we'd been kidnapped, I asked myself over and over again during those long, sleepless nights, "How did I get myself into this mess? What brought me to the deepest part of this jungle?" It was friendship. But it was also my convictions.

In 1992, I met Ingrid while working at the Ministry of Foreign Commerce under minister Juan Manuel Santos Calderón. The two of us assisted him in the area of intellectual properties, so we owe it to him for bringing us together. I was still very young and enjoyed having the opportunity to do something for my country. It also provided us with valuable knowledge of how state bureaucracies functioned and paved the way for us to run a year later for Congress.

Running for Congress was Ingrid's idea, and I thought it would be interesting to join her on this endeavor. At that point, nobody knew us, but we stood up to the challenge despite our anonymity and presented ourselves in the Liberal Party's legislative elections. She topped the list, and I came in second. With the highest number of votes, I was then elected cabinet representative. It was more than a huge accomplishment.

That's where we established our bonds of friendship, sisterhood, and understanding, which we maintained for several years. If we weren't together during the day to day, it was to meet for a cup of coffee, have lunch, or accompany the other to visit our parents—all of this helped keep our friendship alive. That's why it didn't come as a surprise when she called me back in 2001 to ask if we could meet, because she was thinking about abandoning the senate so she could run for president. It seemed like the natural next step, though it would require an enormous effort to achieve such a goal. She invited me to take part in her campaign. After thinking it over for a few months, I joined as chief of staff on September 1, 2001.

I came on board with several others, and we were able to create a solid team and an enriching ideological environment. We began coordinating a series of events that received positive public feedback, and before we knew it, the bid for the presidency was quickly starting to grow. Sadly, it didn't last; most of the campaign members were interested only in presenting a list of candidates for congress's elections. When they realized that this wasn't the objective—reaching the presidency was—they abandoned ship several months later, forcing me to take charge of the campaign as well as its finances. I turned into what's known in Spanish as a *todero*, a do-it-all-yourself worker. Maybe that explains why I ended up in the Florencia airport that day, so Ingrid wouldn't be left all by herself.

11

Escape

It was Simón Bolívar, liberator of Latin America in the nineteenth century, who said that when a person desires freedom intensely enough, he will end up finding it.

The day after we were kidnapped, Ingrid and I asked the guerrillas for a mat to do exercises on and a chess set to pass the time. A few days later, they brought us both items, but we would end up using them for other purposes. Since the mat was black and made out of plastic, it would provide protection from the rain as well as camouflage during our nighttime escape. As for the chess set, the guards grew so used to us losing ourselves in each game that they began paying less attention to us. So while we appeared to be very concentrated on moving our pawns around the board, we were actually devising a plan of escape.

We had been there barely three days when Ingrid and I promised each other that we'd try to escape together at the first opportunity. In retrospect, it was a crazy idea because our guards, who were armed to the teeth, rarely took their eyes off of us. The reality was, they were thrilled to have us as their captives, and it gave them a level of prestige among their bellicose peers.

During those first few weeks, we moved to a new location on a daily basis. We'd go through the same routine every time: we'd get up at the crack of dawn, pack up all of our things, and spend the entire day walking until we had to find a place to pitch our tents for the night. Once we got there, the guerrillas not only had to prepare the site for us but also had to build a small camp for themselves. Then they had to serve us a meal, which required them to find where they could stock up on water and build a bonfire for cooking. At the end of a long day of hiking with their heavy equipment on their backs, they'd be exhausted. We decided that this would be the perfect time for our escape.

One day, about a week after our kidnapping, we arrived at a campsite that we noticed seemed relatively close to a main road. It was around six thirty in the evening and starting to get dark when we decided to make a run for it. But just as we were about to slip off into the jungle, we bumped into a guard and lost our courage to continue with our plan. So we asked where the chonto was to go to the bathroom and headed there instead. That night turned out to be so dark that the escape would have been extra dangerous. When we returned to our barrack hut, we came up with another more detailed plan of escape.

Taking into account that we would have to walk in total darkness once we fled, it was vital that we figure out a way of not getting lost while sticking together at all times. We compiled a short list of things that we would need to take with us: a rope to tie from one to the other around our waists, plastic bags for carrying at least an extra pair of underwear and socks, a T-shirt that could double as a towel, the few toiletries we had (soap, brush, toothpaste), a flashlight, batteries, and extra rope to bind logs together for a floating raft.

We knew that during the night, the guerrillas would check up on us every hour or so. If we placed two large sacks in our beds, it would appear that we were sleeping, and we'd be in the clear until daybreak. This would give us a nine- to ten-hour advantage before they realized that we'd escaped and start looking for us. We decided that we'd go in the FARC uniforms they'd given us as a change of clothes and leave behind our jeans, which we'd stuff with paper so that it looked like we were in bed asleep. We'd also leave our boots—less likely to arouse suspicion—and travel in the sneakers we'd had on the day we were kidnapped.

After a month in captivity, we considered ourselves ready for the big moment. In addition to supplies, we had three sandwiches each, and even some cheese that had been sent to our camp (the only cheese we'd see during those six years of captivity) and two empty water bottles. We had noticed that the guerrillas never carried water on them—too heavy —choosing instead to fill up along the way.

We used our belts as handles for carrying our bags like knapsacks. What we lacked, though, was a machete to slash through the jungle's tall, thick underbrush and clear ourselves a path. I was terrified of the idea of taking it off of one of the guerrillas, simply because if we got caught, it would be the end of us. But Ingrid insisted on its importance and took charge of it herself. She devised a bold and daring scheme: on her way back from bathing, she asked to go to the mess hall where they prepared the food. While she was there, she took advantage of the first distracted person she saw, swiping his machete and concealing it in the dirty pile of clothes she'd brought back with her from bathing. Later on we'd have trouble hiding it and carrying it with us during the hike without hurting ourselves.

Once we had everything ready, we waited for the right moment to escape. Since we were already at the end of March, the month with the brightest nights, we knew we couldn't wait much longer. So on a night when the entire jungle was illuminated by the light of the full moon, we set our plan of escape for the following night. We acted completely normal during the day so that the guerrillas wouldn't suspect a thing. Once it was dark, we went to bed as soon as we could in order to prepare the decoy dummies to leave behind in our beds.

Our luck turned against us when it started pouring around seven o'clock. The night had grown so dark that you couldn't see. But jungle downpours are very loud, and you can hardly hear a thing. So we decided to take our chances and escape in the rain. We tucked our decoys into bed and crept out of the barrack hut. Ingrid went first; I followed behind.

The hardest part was getting past the first level of security without the guards spotting us. Even though it was still raining, we still couldn't risk making a sound. We exited the hut by dragging ourselves along the ground until we reached the chonto. Never in my life had I experienced such a state of nerves and excitement. I sweated profusely and was so alert to everything around me that I must have looked like a cat.

Though the path to the chonto was normally a short one, it took at least an hour to crawl there. But we managed to do so without making a sound or having to turn on the flashlight. We rose to our feet and snuck into the vegetation. Everywhere you turned, there were weeds and trees, and it was hard to orient yourself as to where you were or which direction you were headed. So we kept walking in whatever direction we thought best, using the flashlight every so often to see what we were walking on.

All of a sudden, I tripped on something and rolled onto some kind of clearing. I couldn't help but let out a scream. I quickly shut up and froze with fear. It was nothing serious: I had entangled myself in a root and scratched up my legs a bit. We continued on, walking for hours until we were so exhausted that we decided to stop and rest. We put down our black mat at the edge of a river so we could sit. It was still raining hard, and we were completely soaked. Suddenly we heard something moving next to us, but we couldn't make out what kind of animal it was. I thought it could be a crocodile because you could hear it dragging itself along the ground. We turned on the flashlight but didn't see a thing. When we turned it off, the noises began again, so we decided to get out of there quick. We spotted a river, and though it wasn't very wide, we still didn't have the nerve to cross it. We couldn't tell if it remained this narrow throughout. But we eventually figured out that the river was spiral-shaped and that its banks were full of vegetation. This meant that hiking along the river would be more difficult because we would have to go back into the jungle each time to advance on our trail. Before we knew it, the sun was about to come up, and we had to find a place to hide. Soon we heard the droning of a motorboat: they had already started to search for us.

We remained perfectly still for a good while, almost para-lyzed, trying to not even blink. With the first rays of sunlight, we were shocked to discover that we were standing in thick, muddy water, totally entangled in a type of undergrowth that wrapped around our legs every time we tried to move. We couldn't tell what we were stepping on. And we each tried to cut our way through with the machete, but it was just impossi-ble. By that point, we were emotionally and physically drained and didn't have a drop of energy left in us. Our clothes were still soaked, and we felt cold. Nor had we slept a wink all night from the stress.

The motorboat kept getting closer, and the harder we tried to free ourselves, the more frustrated we became at not being able to move faster. We grew so panicked that we backtracked to the river. There we buried the machete and all our things. We decided to sit down and simply wait for them to pick us up. A few minutes later, a FARC boat, filled with green plantains, pulled up. The guerrilla said, "The comandante is very upset and in a terrible mood. How could you even think of escaping? You could have died out there." We were undoubtedly in terrible state: pale, drenched, and with faces that bore the misery we were in.

When we arrived back at camp, it was evident that the comandante was very upset. Another comandante had arrived to bring supplies, and they were preparing lunch. The only thing that occurred to us to do was to ask for forgiveness and assure them that we wouldn't try it again. They brought us to a place where they gave us buckets of water to bathe with and left us there. It was after noon, and we were starving. They served us a pair of green plantains fresh off the grill. By the end of the day we were moved to a new camp.

After our escape debacle, Ingrid and I found ourselves in a state of despondency and frustration. We had thrown away a golden opportunity. It's amazing: we were able to get through the most difficult part of fooling the guards and leaving the camp, but we weren't capable of crossing the river or trekking far enough into the jungle. I think what scared us that night were those unidentified animal sounds. There was a lot going against us: our fear of the jungle, the rain, the darkness, and not knowing which direction we were headed in.

But we didn't give up and promised each other that we'd try again in a few weeks. Our second attempt, during which we spent three whole days in the jungle, almost cost us our lives. On the second night, we constructed a kind of shelter using the black plastic mat as a roof to protect us from the rain. Once we laid down on the ground, we quickly fell asleep from exhaustion.

A little while later, the two of us awoke to the sound of water, not only from the pelting rain but from flooding. We bolted upright and, in the darkness, gathered whatever we could see of our belongings. The machete was nowhere to be found. The water level was rising rapidly and in minutes had already reached our chests. We panicked and tried to climb the closest tree but couldn't do it. I remember yelling to the heavens, *"Lord, I don't want to die drowning!"*

Despite our desperation and not being able to see a thing, we were able to locate an uphill path that led us to a dry area, where we remained standing until morning. But once again, physical exhaustion and the psychological weight of that dense jungle beat us. We just gave up trying to get out of those inextricable woods.

This time the guerrillas didn't take much pity on us. They were rude and rough. In fact, they put guns to our heads and threatened to kill us if we tried to escape again. After that, they no longer trusted us or gave us a thing, not even a flashlight. Their anger was palpable; they called us a pair of fucking wiseasses. In general, guerrillas don't say much, and when they do, every other word out of their mouth is usually a curse. In response, I told them that if we really were as smart as they thought we were, we wouldn't have become their hostages in the first place. Turns out their ire came from having to report our escape this time around so that they could ask for backup from a search team. After that, we were given a new comandante and a set of guards, and they arrived ready to give us hell. We were chained up for a month.

It was impossible to move. Our ankles were padlocked with a nine-foot-long chain tied around a tree. The only time they unlocked us was to let us go to the bathroom; the rest of the time, we were chained up like animals, even when we slept. I panicked at the thought of what would happen if we were attacked, or if there was another flood, and the guerrillas couldn't unlock us in time. It was the only time I was chained during captivity, and that episode left an indelible mark on me. It was a barbaric act. There's no other way to describe it. I was furious and began feeling like I had to be the most miserable person on earth and that those guerrillas were the most detestable human beings I could have ever imagined meeting.

Yet even in that state, I was able to control my anguish and remain silent. I think it was after this that my attitude toward Ingrid began to change. It annoyed me that on our second escape attempt, she completely lost it in front of a wasps nest in pure daylight. I remember exactly how it happened: in order to cross a dried-up brook, we had to duck beneath a bridge barely four feet tall. She was about three feet ahead of me when she bumped into the nest and ran out of there screaming. I caught up with her standing on a path and flailing her arms in all directions, desperately trying to free herself from a swarm of wasps. It was the middle of the day; someone was liable to pass by and hear her screams. I implored my friend to calm down and stop screaming; that she was only making the wasps angrier. Then I told her to slowly take off her jacket and place it in on the ground beside her, and the wasps would go away. That's what she did, and she was finally left in peace. But someone had to get the jacket away from the wasps. So when I slowly got close to it in order to pick it up, that's when they must have stung my feet. Unfortunately, I was wearing sneakers, not boots, and a few hours later my feet swelled up so much, I could hardly walk.

On top of the rage and powerlessness of being prisoners again, when we returned from our second attempt at escaping, we received news that Ingrid's father had died of cardiac and respiratory disease. Gabriel Betancourt Mejía had been a government minister. We read it in a newspaper that a guerrilla had given us, and it filled us with an inconsolable and profound sadness. In spite of this, the guerrillas didn't commiserate and chained us right up.

Because I couldn't walk or move much in those chains, I spent a lot of time praying. I asked them to bring me a Bible, and they did, along with some creams. After breakfast and lunch, which usually consisted of an agua de panela, I would read the sacred Scriptures aloud so that Ingrid could distract herself a bit by thinking about something else. She was so morose that I had to insist she make an effort to keep on living if only for the sake of her teenage children, Lorenzo and Mélanie.

That's when we began a nine-day-fast to protest our chains. We prayed with the rosary morning, noon, and night, along with nine nights of prayer for her father's soul. His death had also affected me, and I relived the pain I had experienced less than a year before when my father passed away. Ingrid was in profound mourning, and seeing her suffer so much disheartened me even more.

Being chained during that difficult time of mourning affected us so, that something inside of us began to change. Each day dragged on into the next with a gloomy monotony that was hard to bear. That's when the silence between us began to take over. We hardly spoke to each other or said hello. We would just read the Bible and comment on what we had read. Once that was finished, it felt like there was nothing left to talk about.

12

The Unraveling
of a Friendship

Without any hope of salvation, the two of us lost all motivation, and we began drowning in our own sadness. In all human dramas, there are different approaches to confronting a dilemma. And in our case, without giving it much thought, we both chose silence.

Though we never spoke about it, I imagine that each of us blamed the other for foiling our two attempts at escaping. We never discussed what went wrong, much less planned a new mode of escape after that. All that misdirected pain ended up creating a wall between us, and we became like those couples who become total strangers once communication has completely failed them. It's not like I could tell you that there was a specific event that severed our friendship; it was more like a slow distancing in light of our circumstances.

I wasn't really sure what else to say to Ingrid while she was mourning her father. I tried to liven her up by inviting her to pray and read the Bible. But I was also sad and having a hard time. I couldn't help but think, as I still do today, that I had sacrificed myself by going with her on that trip. It turned out to be a totally useless decision, for what good did it do if today we're so distant from each other? I couldn't understand not being able to maintain a certain level of understanding. And being in chains to boot, it felt as though we had begun a slow descent into death.

I was furious with myself for having followed her on that dangerous trip to San Vicente del Caguán. But I couldn't complain about it to her. I didn't have the right to. I was also having trouble digesting the sight of her in pain. She had always been so strong and determined, and it was upsetting to watch her falling apart. I even believe that she wanted to die. She grew from being a role model for me to someone who represented death, becoming extremely apathetic and bitter. It got so bad, we weren't even able to maintain a conversation about that hell we were living. It seems to me that all of this created a barrier between us that, to this day, we haven't been able to surmount.

Our differences in character manifested themselves even more in an extreme situation like that. There was nothing to spark a conversation between us or bring us together for a reason. I believe that Ingrid, to a certain degree, is a more political being than I am: you are either with her or against her. I, on the other hand, can disagree with someone but not consider him my enemy.

For both of us, life together became practically impossible, and the comandante who watched over us decided to place us in separate barrack huts. Not wanting to be rudely turned away, I didn't make any attempts at getting close to her. So I waited for her to pay me a visit when she wanted to. She'd come at least once a month, and with the rosary, we would sit and pray for her father.

The comandantes would remind us now and again that we were both hostages and that we should be helping each other. I thought it was absurd that they tried to involve themselves in our personal matters, as if we were incapable of ironing out our own differences.

One day I asked the guerrillas for a dictionary to pass the time with. But much to my dismay, when they finally brought it to the camp, Ingrid wouldn't let me use it. She also made me suffer when she threw me out of the French class she would give every so often to the other hostages. Ingrid was born in Colombia but grew up in France and was a dual citizen of both countries. The amazing thing about her was that she seemed resentful of the fact that I liked to spend my time in a constructive manner. Her behavior also seemed strange to the guerrillas, and they began giving us our things separately so that I wouldn't be left empty handed. During that period, I

learned a lot about human relations. And over time, and especially when we had to join an even larger group of hostages,
the way they chose to behave mattered less and less to me.

There certainly wasn't anything to justify the abysmal distancing that Ingrid and I underwent, especially after everything
we had been through together. But people's reasoning and
emotions don't always manifest themselves in the same way—
or follow similar trains of thought, for that matter. That's why
human relations are so complex. And during periods of hard-
ship, it's even more difficult to completely understand what
nests in the hearts and minds of others.

Unfortunately, in the end, all that remains of this sad chapter is the bad taste in my mouth.

13

Solitude

When I found myself alone for the first time in my hut, after they'd separated me from Ingrid, I was overcome with three distinct feelings. The first was need, in terms of realizing that now I was alone and had to manage the best I could— which to a degree reminded me of my life before captivity as an independent person. The second: peace, for having my own space brought a new sense of tranquility. And the third: solitude. I felt I had the strength to tolerate life as a hostage, but it ended up being harder than I thought.

It didn't take very long for me to create a routine, which is crucial when confronting a situation like that. I'd awake at four in the morning, go to the chonto, wash myself, and then return to my hut to fix it up. During that period, they had given me a small radio. It had poor reception, but it could pick up a transmission from the southern city of El Doncello, Caquetá. Sometimes I could even tune in a local 6:00 a.m. broadcast of the national news. I'd sit and listen until 6:10, then go fetch my tinto—the black coffee they gave us every morning. I would read and reread a few of the magazines the guerrillas had given us until around 7:30, when they brought breakfast. After that I would walk around my hut for an hour or two—sometimes even four—until it was time for lunch. I took advantage of my walking time to pray on my rosary and reflect on all kinds of things. I thought a lot about what my life would be like when I was free again. After lunch I'd wash my dishes, brush my teeth, and then rest a bit.

Close to 2:00 in the afternoon, I'd walk some more or sit down to sew. Around 4:00, I'd prepare my clothes in case the female guerrilla, who brought me my food, should offer to take me to the river. For a full thirty minutes, I could delight in swimming upriver, using the briskest strokes I had against the current; then I'd just let myself go and allow it to take me back down again. It was without a doubt my favorite part of the day. With my arms wide open, I'd float along, looking up at the sky and feeling completely free. Those moments filled me with energy and helped keep me in good physical condition. Back then I was still under forty, svelte (I had always kept myself in shape), and with a face that hadn't changed much since I was younger. But my days of swimming in the river were finished once that giant snake appeared, and the comandante forbade me from going in.

By five I was dressed again and ready for dinner, which usually consisted of an agua de panela with a piece of *cancharina*: a puff pastry made from wheat flour. Afterward, I'd wash my dishes, brush my teeth, and this would conclude my day's activities. During that period in my captivity, I still hadn't figured out how to install the radio antenna and couldn't find any programs to listen to in the evening. Without much left to do, and since it was already dark by then, I'd just crawl under my blanket.

It didn't take long for this extreme state of solitude to take full effect. I spent most of my day in silence, except to greet and say thank you to the guerrilla who brought me breakfast or lunch. I had to eat all my meals alone, so there wasn't anyone I could talk to or discuss what I had heard on the radio that morning. There weren't newspapers for me to read, and I felt completely alienated from the rest of the world. I plunged into a state of loneliness and absolute monotony. There were nights where I couldn't sleep, and when it rained, I'd lie there in fear that the river nearby would overflow. Each time I went to bathe, I'd check to see how high the river was, to calm my nerves. I can't begin to tell you how terrifying the jungle can be during a storm; I'd even dare to say that the thunder and lighting could be as scary as the sounds of falling bombs.

In the midst of that absolute solitude, I did all I could to keep my spirits high. I tried to keep track of the days. This proved difficult to do, since every day in the jungle looks and feels exactly like the others.

I lived confined to a world devoid of sound, where I didn't speak to anyone and got used to people not talking to me. One day while I was washing clothes, the comandante came over to tell me something. Instead of responding, I kept doing what I was doing and didn't even bat an eyelash. He came closer, calling me by my name, and still I didn't answer. He repeated it several more times until he lost his patience and yelled, "Clara!" I was completely out of it; my body was present, but my mind was somewhere else. His scream startled me, and I turned around to look at him. I can't even remember what he wanted, but that incident demonstrates what can happen to the mind in complete isolation. It was pure psychological abuse, a form of violence difficult to comprehend if you've never suffered through it. I was a human in complete desolation.

Today I still ask myself where I found the strength to cope, especially since I'd grown up in such a warm family environment, where I was my father's favorite and always the center of attention. From the crib, to law school, and beyond, I had always been lavished with affection. Captivity was an especially hostile environment for someone like me, and the isolation began eating me up inside. Even the comandante must have noticed I was in bad shape. He came up with the idea of building a track for me to run and exercise on. It was circular, almost hexagonal in shape, and to one side they installed a set of bars for flexes, and on another, some boards for doing push-ups. So every afternoon at four o'clock, I'd go to the track to exercise.

I'm completely certain that the comandante, like the rest of the guerrillas in the camp, were aware of the psychological damage being done and the pain I was in. Months later, in fact, before they moved us to another camp, they offered their verbal apologies *in the name of the organization*.

14

Fasting

Man does not live by bread alone.

I was able to create a daily routine to keep my body active and fit. But my mind, heart, and soul were still stuck on my family.

When you consider the idea of food in the middle of a jungle—the scarcity of it and its proper storage—the dishes they managed to prepare for us were decent, and I can't say I disliked them. But without anyone to share a meal with, I didn't have an appetite, I was so depressed. In those conditions, it was relatively easy to start a fast that lasted twenty-one days. Each morning I'd eat an *arepa,* a round cornmeal cake that's popular in Colombia, with an agua de panela, and that was it. It was coming up on one year since my kidnapping. During all that time, I hadn't received a message or heard any news about my family. And when I was able to catch something on the radio about our hostage situation, there was no mention of my name. It felt as though the jungle had swallowed up even the memory of me.

I thought that I should do something in protest. My fast lasted from February 2 to February 22—the exact one-year anniversary. This hunger strike was the second major fast I had completed. The first had been for nine days with Ingrid when we objected to being in chains; thanks to the strike, they finally removed them. Another time I tried to start one, but I was able to resist only a few days. The hardest part, at least for me, is the first three days. The key is to think about anything but food. The mere thought of it depletes your will.

What motivated me to fast? The need to feel closer to God. In biblical terms, I felt the need to please Him, to ask for His attention, clemency, protection, and guidance. I came to the conclusion that I had been made to suffer through this bitter experience for a reason: to evolve as a human being.

During the three-week fast, I was able to accomplish various things. I found that I could fortify my willpower while also letting go of my attachment to material things. In a practical sense, I became a problem for the comandantes, since they were under strict orders not to let me die of hunger. They didn't have any choice but to accept my fast, though they saw it as an act of rebellion. And that's exactly how I wanted it to look; I was going against their norms.

Due to the fact that I had been able to read some of the guerrillas' internal regulations written in a notebook, I knew that they had to show consideration for their hostages' religious and personal beliefs. So to avoid any retaliation, I presented my fast as if it were a religious practice that they should respect—and they did, albeit unwillingly. I'd always inform them of my fast's start and finish dates, which also served to reinforce my own commitment. But even during those set dates, the guerrillas still kept bringing me my food so that nobody could ever blame them for not supplying me with meals.

If on some occasion I was made to sit with the other hostages during meals, I wouldn't serve myself any food and left it in the pot so that someone else could have it. I thought it would be in poor taste to serve myself and then just leave it, since I had been taught by my parents to never waste food.

I fasted an additional five times over the next five years until my release. What did I accomplish with all of this? Apparently, not much. But I felt that at least in a blunt but respectful way, I was reminding the guerrillas that what they were doing was wrong.

Fasting is a trying experience under any circumstance, and in the jungle it's even worse. At any moment, you could be called on a weeklong trek, and when you haven't eaten well and don't have the strength, walking for hours at a time becomes a superhuman act. Also, when you're a hostage in a jungle, without any material possessions to distract you, food and the act of eating become far more important than in normal, everyday life. So by giving it up on my own, I was able to learn a lot about myself and my nature.

I also learned things about the others around me. When I was in the company of my fellow hostages, I noticed that my fasting gave them more respect for me. This was true with the guerrillas, too, because for them eating is essential. I was aware that my behavior was impacting everyone. As a free woman today, I still receive letters of admiration from high-ranking church clergymen for renouncing food during my time as a hostage, something they imagine as being even more difficult to do under my stressful circumstance.

All of these tests of willpower brought me closer to God in ways I could have never imagined. I got to the point where I began having very strange dreams. But as incomprehensible as they were, those visions left me with the hope that I'd reunite with my family and be free again one day.

During my last three months of captivity, I was filled with an inner peace and an inexplicable serenity that allowed me to face my newfound freedom with integrity. But that ordeal came with its repercussions. I started suffering from gastritis, or inflammation of the stomach. On several occasions, I had powerful stomachaches, high fevers, and the chills. Even today I still suffer stomach pains. I know now that I was simply letting my heart lead me, and all that effort only helped strengthen my faith. And so it was worthwhile.

15

Faith

Faith is a virtue. It's a deep concept and can sometimes be difficult to explain. But when certain elements are brought together in a life, you can reach it. First your heart has to be open to it, followed by a certain type of demeanor from your mind and soul. After that, it all starts to come together. As it says in the book of Hebrews (11:1, 6): "Now faith is the substance of things hoped for, the evidence of things not seen . . . But without faith it is impossible to please Him: or he that cometh to God must believe that He is, and that He is a rewarder of them that diligently seek him."

How did I develop this virtue? When I was born, I was baptized and introduced into the Catholic faith. I studied at a school run by Spanish nuns where for twelve years I regularly attended mass and took religion and catechism classes. In fact, I became friends with a group of girls who liked to go on hikes in Bogotá's surrounding mountains to pray on our rosaries and conduct minifasts for the Virgin Mary. When I enrolled at Our Lady of the Rosary University, a very traditional Bogotá institution, I still attended mass whenever I could.

Like a majority of Colombians, I'm a practicing Catholic. But my faith was put to the test during captivity, and it's reached a level of importance in my life that I never could have imagined before. Each and every day during those six years when I was deprived of my liberty, my faith kept me alive. I'm convinced that I wouldn't have survived that nightmare if it weren't for my deep religious convictions. During the initial stages of the kidnapping, I decided to accept all that was happening to me and hold myself back from asking God to give me strength. Other hostages, in comparison, having reached the point of total desperation, began viewing suicide as their only option for putting an end to the hell we were living. I never thought about taking my own life; for me, existence is a gift from God, and it's not in our hands to dispose of.

I had always wanted to read the entire Bible, and captivity allowed me all the time in the world to finally do so. The guerrillas actually supplied me with a copy within just a few weeks of my asking for it. Each day I'd set a number of pages as a goal. Then I'd sit down to read them in seven to eight hours. By the end of the month, I'd already finished it, something I considered a great accomplishment. It was like going on some exotic trip you've always dreamed of taking and that you can do only once in a lifetime.

Later on I had to leave my Bible behind with my few other belongings when we had to quickly clear the camp. But I was able to bring a copy of the New Testament that I'd received as a gift from a fellow hostage who had been kidnapped because he was a soldier in the Colombian army. I cared for it like a prized possession until the day I was freed; I even made a cloth pouch to keep it in. From the used toothpaste tubes I collected, I created a book cover of sorts to ward off the insects. I'd cut the plastic tubes open down the middle and spread them over the Bible's cover so the ants would be deterred by the toothpaste remnants.

I'd often go back and reread it, concentrating on certain passages or verses that had piqued my attention. I enjoyed the parables the most; as a little girl, I was always told of their importance. There were three that meant the most to me during captivity. The first was the one about having a talent, because I'm aware that when you have a certain gift, you should find it in your heart to help others with it. Then there was the parable about the lost sheep, because for me the FARC are like the lost sheep of humanity's flock. We should take responsibility for making them understand the most basic of human rights: the right to your own life, and to one with dignity. For this reason, it doesn't come as a surprise that the government of Colombian president Álvaro Uribe rewards guerrillas who free hostages with a plan to help them change and rebuild their lives. This progressive initiative has enticed thousands of rebels to lay down their arms.

The parable about Jesus' miracle of turning water into wine during the wedding at Cana also ran through my head again and again. I was painfully aware that I was living in a high-risk situation where I could die at any moment. That's why, with the passing of the days, weeks, months, and eventually years, I began to accept and develop a great deal of tolerance for the reality I was living. There was nothing I could do but learn to be patient. This is the lesson that I stress most to my son, Emmanuel. I've written these words for him and for his generation so that when he's older he can reflect on this message. It's important to learn how to be patient in life because it allows us to build on our own character so that over time we can begin showing our very best to the world, just like at the wedding in Cana, where they left the best wine for last.

Beyond reading the Bible, I also spent a lot of time praying, convinced that somewhere in that enormous jungle, the Almighty was able to hear me. My favorite time was at daybreak when there was absolute silence. Nobody could interrupt my prayers, and it seemed like the best way to pass the time during those dark hours. It was ideal for meditating; it was like I had God's ear all to myself. It brought back memories of what it was like talking to my father or a loved one again.

Sometimes, during my daytime showers, I sang songs to the Virgin Mary. But in reality, I couldn't remember all the lyrics, since I'd learned them back when I was in school. But it didn't matter: just the act of singing lifted my spirits. Then there were times I'd wake up at five in the morning and sing to the Virgin Mary while it was still dark out. "As you walk through life, you're never alone / Fight for a new world, fight for the truth / Come walk with us, Saint Mary / Come, come walk with us." The other song I liked to sing went: "Jesus Christ left me eager, His word filled me with light / I couldn't go back to seeing the world without feeling what Jesus felt anymore."

I know that the military hostages at our camp liked when I sang because it made them feel less alone. And for the most part, the guerrillas never said a word. Naturally, there was someone who didn't appreciate my singing and let me know it by whistling at me one day. But he eventually got over it. Another time, one of the guerrillas, who seemed to be a polite and decent young man, was picking up the pots and pans from our meal. He asked me, "Clara, but who are you singing to?" I told him that I was singing to my father, to God, and that I'd been told to love God as if He were my own father.

He replied, "Believe me, if God really existed, you wouldn't be in captivity."

I answered him by saying that it wasn't God's will to make me a captive but the will of his comandantes, who aren't on a clear path in life. I ended our conversation by telling him that one day when he needed help, because eventually he would, he should ask God to show him the way.

• • •

Sometime in 2006, I got hold of a radio on which I could pick up a signal for World Catholic Radio in the evenings. I just loved listening to it and I especially enjoyed a children's catechism show they aired. Sometimes I would catch the pre-recorded talks of Pope John Paul II, and this moved me a great deal. I'd been fond of him since he was first made Pope in 1978, and I liked that he was an athlete before he joined the clergy. It made me remember when he visited Colombia twenty years back, and I was in a youth group that organized his welcome to our country. Because I had also read most of his books, hearing him speak from my little lost corner of the jungle seemed magical. The radio station kept up with the Pope's activities, and in 2005, when it reported that he had died, I remember being saddened like so many other Catholics around the world.

I also followed the talks of the new Pope, Benedict XVI. One of the first books I was given when I was freed was a book written by this very Pope about Jesus of Nazareth. I read it while I was recovering from an operation I had undergone, and the book's theme, which concerns man's freedom, drew me in for obvious reasons. The Holy Father analyzes Jesus' life, as well as the Torah, and quotes a passage from Saint Paul's Letter to the Galatians:

"For you were called to freedom . . . only do not turn your freedom into an opportunity for the flesh . . . Liberty is liberty for doing good, liberty that allows itself to be led by the spirit of God. Yes, evil exists and God exists. But evil comes from man's poor use of free will." I thought about the FARC rebels and how irresponsible they were for using arms to kidnap and force people into captivity—to take away their liberty.

There wasn't one moment of my captivity where I lost my faith in God and His profound compassion. Also, I can't forget all those people around the world who prayed for me and for my son, and who today let me know that they did when they greet me on the street. A few weeks ago, a beautiful eight-year-old girl approached me with a gift of a tiny Virgin of Guadalupe medallion and said, "Clara, I want you to know that my family and I prayed for you and that we're happy that you're with Emmanuel again. God bless you today, tomorrow, and always."

16

Doubt and Anxiety

Besides feeling lonely and isolated, the other two enemies that a kidnapped person must fight every day are doubt and anxiety. Doubt is when you lack certainty and you fear your uncertain future, whereas anxiety is a state of agitation that doesn't allow you peace.

In our everyday life, anxiety can be provoked by events such as the death of a loved one, losing a job, or moving to a new city. Try to imagine, then, the anxiety produced when you lose everything in a single moment. When you're a hostage, nothing is certain: not your meals, where you'll sleep, what you're going to do the next day, or if you'll even live to see it. Captivity is the brutal stripping away of everything you've had, your loved ones, and your daily routine. You lack any control over your life and your surroundings. All that's left is your own being. And that can be found only when you're ready to face yourself—nowhere else. It's no surprise that this state can cause agitation, uncertainty, and unease in people. So when it's prolonged for years, the suffering is unimaginable.

You have two choices when you're a hostage: let yourself die or fight for your life. When you opt to survive, and rid yourself of insane and morbid thoughts, you have to work at it every day without fail to truly achieve it. You have to be creative and take advantage of the few resources you have around you, whether they're real or in your head. And those small but constant efforts end up making a difference over time. Naturally there are moments of sadness and confusion where you can't hold back the tears. But the important part is trying to curb those times so that you can be stronger in the long run. To do this, a person has to work a lot on herself or himself. For you can't forget the famous adage "God helps those who help themselves."

To keep doubt at bay, you must look for ways of finding out what is happening in the world. Information becomes vital to your survival. Before I was kidnapped, I always kept myself informed through newspapers, magazines, and television. But in the jungle, I had none of this. Every once in a while, I'd get an outdated copy of a publication to read. Then there were periods when I could avidly listen to the news on the radio. But during those first two years, when I hardly received any outside news, my world was a living hell.

During the four years that followed, I passed through

stages. First, my complete fascination with listening to the radio, even if for just a few minutes a day. It allowed me to feel somewhat in the know. Next I went through a period of total isolation until the end of 2005. And during the last stage of captivity, when we were allowed to have a radio and actually listen to the news a couple times a day, I was able to keep myself highly informed.

Months after the cruel separation from my baby, the guerrillas gave me a radio as a palliative against my heartbreak and loneliness. That was when I learned to concoct an antenna using an unraveled scouring pad. The stainless steel extended to about thirty feet and I attached a rock to one end for anchoring. With some help from the police and military hostages, I was able to throw it over the treetops. Eventually I was able to get the antenna very high up in the trees and could listen to England's BBC, Spain's Radio Exterior de España, and Radio France Internationale, though it would work only for a few minutes a day.

But of course the news and radio programs we paid most attention to were on the Colombian stations Caracol Radio and RCN. In the mornings and late afternoons, we'd listen to *La Luciérnaga (Firefly)* or *Hora 20 (20th Hour)* on Caracol Radio or *El Cocuyo (Lightning Bug)* on RCN Radio. These shows would talk about current events while mixing in some humor. Sometimes we could pick up W Radio, my favorite Bogotá station before I was kidnapped, though it could be light on the news-talk format at times. But the mere fact of being able to listen to it in the jungle made me feel a lot better. My fellow hostages preferred their own local stations, so between all the different programs we caught, I was able to listen to at least an hour and one-half of news a day during my last two years of captivity.

I liked to discuss the news with the other hostages and hear their thoughts. There were plenty of times that I thought they were overly pessimistic and preferred not having to hear what they were saying. But this was also good for me because it balanced out my tendency to be overly optimistic and trusting. After a while, I got to know the other hostages so well that I knew what they were going to say even before they said it. Nonetheless, I still paid attention.

It was only natural that we'd be particularly interested in following the radio programs that aired messages for the hostages, such as *La Carrilera (The Railroad)* on RCN at five o'clock in the morning and *Las voces del secuestro* (*Voices from Captivity*) on Radio Caracol every Sunday morning from two to six. The shows broadcast messages from family and friends to the hostages, and hearing it was very comforting for our souls. We ended up getting to know the family members of the other hostages pretty well, so that they started feeling like part of our own family. Other times, friends would share candid stories and anecdotes about their lives that we found entertaining, along the lines of, "Hi, Juancho, we went to a barbeque at the country house on Friday, and guess what? Patty was there. Man, you missed out; she looked totally hot! We missed you. I hope that the next time around, you'll be able to join us, Lord willing.

Hugs." Then there were the messages directed to certain gentlemen at our camp from their so-called "good female friends." I especially had fun listening to those and am sure that they left the men content for a while. Sometimes the spontaneous messages from friends outnumbered the ones from family members, who would complain about these "other people" taking up too much air time. But I really enjoyed what the friends had to say, and it seemed that, in general, so did the other hostages.

There were the messages that moved me the most, like the one from the director of my secondary school that had been published in the Colombian newspaper *El Tiempo* and which my mother read on the radio:

My beloved and always remembered Clara Lety,

It's not the first time that I try to write you, but today, All Kings Day, I'll try again. Though this magic night has already passed here in Spain, I know you're all still living through it in Colombia. The Kings visited us from the Orient tonight, and it's especially lovely to see the children full of hope and wanting to make their dreams realities. I ask the King of our heart to make so many people's only wish come true: to hug one of the most beautiful, loving, and brave daughters our school has seen, and where we all already knew you'd grow up to become an innovative woman who fights for and defends the justice of all. The truth is, I'm very proud of you.

My mother would often send me her own loving messages that she recorded with her own music in the background:

For my beloved Clara Lety,

When things happen for their own reasons, we remain thinking about the possible reasons and analyzing them . . . May God bless you. I love you. Your mother.

Daughter of my soul,

I also trust in you and in my Lord and His blessings. I trust that life will be normal again, along with the peace and harmony of our beloved country. I'm grateful to God for giving me a daughter like you. Your mother.

To Clara Lety,

We think about you and love you with all our hearts. Receive the blessings that all who can send to you. Your mother.

Sometimes it was hard for me to listen to the entire program, as hearing other people's problems only added to all the weight on our souls. Many of the persons sending messages were sad and depressed themselves, criticizing the government and the FARC. So it was best for us take a little distance from it sometimes and give it less importance, so that it wouldn't bring us down even more.

It's a good thing that I eventually got my own shortwave radio and could switch between those programs and the ones on the Global Catholic Radio Network, along with the sports shows. I actually began following the Formula 1 races in which Colombia's national hero, race car driver Juan Pablo Montoya, would compete.

But in any case, the radio programs dedicated to speaking directly to the hostages accomplished a very important mission. After I was freed, I visited several of their studios to thank the journalists and to encourage them to keep doing what they'd been doing. I also wanted to say hello to the people still in captivity and show solidarity with their suffering that I know all too well. That's why when I speak to them I send brief but positive messages filled with the happiness I now feel. I want to convey to them that freedom is something that can be attained. So for as long as it takes, they should keep holding out for it. I also dedicate to them a few songs that meant a lot to me, such as "Esta Vida" by Jorge Celedón and Jimmy Zambrano; it was the song they greeted us with the day the helicopters came to take us home:

> I like the smell of the morning; I like my first sip of
>   coffee.
> To feel how the sun comes to my window and fills me
>   with its presence.
> A beautiful morning.
> I like to listen to the peace of the mountains,
> Ponder the colors of sunset,
> Feel my feet in the beach's sand and taste the sweetness of
>   sugarcane.

When I kiss my lady, I know that time moves quick, wants
to scratch me off its list,
But I tell her, Oh . . . how beautiful life is!

"Esta Vida" is an example of a *vallenato*, a popular form of folk music that comes primarily from Colombia's northeastern coastal region. *Vallenato* means "born in the valley," and historically, that valley is located between two mountain ranges known as the Sierra Nevada de Santa Marta and the Serranía de Perijá.

"Con la gente que me gusta," by Los Arciniegas is another song I dedicated to them one morning. It says:

With the people I like I talk until dawn with,
We share sunrises, words, laughs, and moons.
With the people I like, I spend sleepless nights . . .
I like those people who squeeze your hand tight,
And without doubt, when they greet you, I like people . . .

In late 2008, I met with the army soldiers who were rescued along with Ingrid six months after my own release. You can imagine my surprise when they thanked me for my radio messages, saying that it touched them deeply while they were still in captivity. I laughed and said, "Well, that's what they were aiming to do!"

The other enemy you have to battle in captivity is anxiety. It leads many hostages to chain-smoke, overeat, or fall into something equally damaging: a sedentary life. In order for the anxiety not to consume you, you have to make an effort to be creative and disciplined, setting a daily agenda and following it through however best you can. In the jungle, it's easy to flag, especially when nobody, not even the other hostages, cares to comment or worry about anyone. It's up to you to decide whether to spend your days staring at the roof or using them for a more constructive purpose.

Being locked up with limited movement generates anxiety as well. It's always been important for me to exercise, but in the jungle it became an act of survival—almost a question of life or death—precisely because it helped ease the tension and anxiety that gripped me; that's why I tried to walk each day for at least forty-five minutes even if it was just in a circle around my barrack hut. My Lord, there were days I even walked for four hours around that little place! When I could, I jogged, especially when I was at the campsite where they'd built me a track. On average, I exercised five to six times a week, sometimes even daily.

Afterward came the long-awaited time of the day when I could bathe. I enjoyed it tremendously, most of all when they allowed me to swim. Later on even just the act of cleaning myself outdoors with a bucket of water filled me with peace. First I would wash my clothes, and then I'd wash myself. Those were the happiest moments of my day, and I would sing and thank God for them. In order to put my clothes on, I would rustle up a curtain made out of leaves, plastic bags, or towels—anything that would afford me a little privacy. Since these were my moments of tranquility, I always tried to bathe alone, and did so probably about four-fifths of the time.

But other times, especially during those long treks, we had to bathe in a group. They'd send us off in turns to wash in the river, and even then I still tried to be one of the last to go. Since we arrived from the hikes soaked in sweat, the majority of the time we went into the river with our clothes on so we could wash our uniforms simultaneously. One of the other military hostages once accused me in front of the guerrillas of not wanting to cooperate with the others by not bathing with everybody else. I found this hilarious and told him that I wasn't afraid to bathe alone and that the army surely taught him how to bathe alone—and to respect a woman's right to privacy as well. The truth is, the comandantes never complained once about this habit of mine.

In general, after I bathed, I'd start to feel hungry and would gladly eat whatever they gave me, although I passed through periods without the slightest of appetites. The food was very simple, and I was always amazed by the fact that the pots in which they brought us our food always looked clean. To me this was very important. I thought it was decent of the FARC to maintain this custom of cleanliness. When we were all in a group, they'd normally carry out three big pots to serve all of us; even Emmanuel when he was still at my side.

For breakfast they'd bring a pot with arepas (the round cornmeal cakes), another with soup, and a third with hot chocolate—sometimes plain, sometimes with milk in it. Lunch consisted of white rice accompanied by beans, lentils, or string beans. They'd also bring another pot with our drink in it, which was usually agua de panela. And at night they'd serve us white rice and spaghetti.

Every once in a while, they'd offer us some meat that came from the mountainside; one time it was monkey and jaguar meat, which I found very hard to chew. They would often serve us *babilla* (meat from a small crocodile), which the guerrillas call *cachirrí*. It has a delicious texture and tastes a bit like lobster. Sometimes at night they'd offer us canned tuna fish and sardines or a fish they had caught that day in the river.

A lot of times, the food was too greasy for me to eat; even the hot chocolate. I especially remember that twice a year the comandante would prepare *empanadas*—fried patties filled with meat, potato, egg, vegetable, or a combination thereof, popular in Colombia—or tamales; we'd each get two. And every so often, they'd surprise us with a special drink, such as *avena*, an oatmeal-based beverage made with milk or water; *colada*, a corn-based drink, popular in Ecuador and Colombia, that's mixed with flour, water, and milk, and can be served with either salt or sugar; or rice milk.

During my last year of captivity, we had two very special meals. One was on December 8, 2007, for the Feast of the Immaculate Conception, when they gave each of us half a grilled chicken, which in the jungle is a sheer delicacy. They also prepared a creamy Colombian dessert called *natilla*, made of milk, cinnamon, coconut, and sugarcane, and a beverage made of fermented *masato* (yucca, rice, corn, or pineapple), rice milk, and sugarcane. On another occasion, also close to the day I was freed, they served us an oven-baked suckling pig and a type of mountain pig they called *cajuche*, served with a side of yucca. The portions were so enormous that I couldn't finish them, and the leftovers lasted me for a few more meals. So that the food I kept wouldn't spoil, I'd stick the dishes into a bag filled with water, which would preserve it well for a day.

We hostages had a habit that was a bit masochistic: we'd sit around describing to each other, in great detail, the tastes of our favorite foods from back home. It could be torturous. For instance, I loved to talk about *ajiaco* with chicken, which is a traditional potato-based soup from Bogotá's savanna. But given the fact that it's made from four types of potatoes that grow only in a cold climate, I would see it only in my imagination. We'd recall aloud what this soup experience tasted like: the corn, the capers, the cream, the bread, the avocado, and the *curuba* juice to wash it down—along with other mouth-watering temptations that we'd never be able to eat in the jungle. And as if that weren't painful enough, we'd also name our favorite restaurants and describe the special dishes on the menus. I loved reminiscing about how they prepared certain dishes, so they'd be fresh in my mind when I was free again to devour them.

During those culinary conversations, we'd also comment on the food the guerrillas prepared. It was a way to pass the time, and we'd critique each meal as if we were fancy food critics. Was it served too hot or too cold? Too salty or bland? Was the rice prepared well? One problem you'd run into when cooking rice in the jungle was that you'd wind up with damp-flavored grains due to the high humidity. To compensate, they'd oversalt the food to hide the stale taste. They'd also oversalt the meats to prevent spoilage. Though meat was a prized possession, I'd often give away my servings to whoever wanted it. I preferred the fish they'd offer us, especially when it was cooked simply. Another problem of eating in the jungle is the flies on your food, especially the beverages, which irked me a great deal. Some of the hostages, though, weren't bothered by them; in fact, they even swallowed them. I never reached that point.

When I returned to Bogotá after being freed, the first meal my family prepared for me at my brother's house was a delicious ajiaco soup with chicken. And I loved watching my son, Emmanuel, enjoying it as much as I did.

17

Pastimes

How does one measure the passing of time in captivity?

Before I was kidnapped, I was a slave to time. I tried to organize my days as best I could and even bought books to help me find ways to do it better. When I returned home after an intense day, completely exhausted, I went to bed feeling that time wasn't allowing me to do all the things that needed to get done. I was constantly complaining to friends and colleagues about my lack of time.

In captivity I was suddenly faced with having all the time in the world for myself, but apparently not being able to do a thing to take advantage of it. Never had I experienced so intensely the sensation of wasting time as during the first months of captivity. It was an existential conflict so horrid that

I could see my entire life wasting away in front of my eyes. I felt like I was burying my youth in that jungle.

I couldn't do anything productive. I also couldn't allow myself to think that I was sick and needed to get better. It wasn't enough to have a daily routine with a series of healthy habits, such as waking up early, straightening up, exercising, washing myself, my clothes, thinking about my family—yes, all of this was an undeniable help. But the state I was in, stripped of everything, made it difficult to keep myself busy and use my time constructively.

I soon realized that this exceptional case demanded something else that came from within. In an effort to stay busy, I asked for a notebook and pen, which both ran out in no time. I wrote nonstop; in the first year alone, I filled more than eight hundred-page notebooks, singled spaced. I even got to the point where I started writing on the toilet paper wrapping. In diary style, I wrote all sorts of things, anything that entered my mind. When I was alone, I'd write about the news I'd heard on the radio, or I'd reread passages in the Bible so I could summarize them. It was a diary about everything that I was seeing and feeling. When we had to move to another camp, they were much too heavy to carry, and I was left with no choice but to burn them. I'd go back to the writing again later on—that is, until they stopped giving me notebooks because they were annoyed with all the letters I was writing to Manuel Marulanda and the other members of the FARC secretariat, begging them to free my son.

While it lasted, I wrote as much as I possibly could. I also dabbled in painting. A bunch of times, I sat down and copied word for word from an English-Spanish dictionary they had loaned me. Or I entertained myself by going over multiplication tables and the calculations for square roots. In retrospect, these activities proved to be great brain exercises, and that's how I'd spend a good portion of my mornings. I even prepared a script for the next proof-of-life video they might ask me to do. It was a message to my mother that I'd update and rewrite now and again where I spoke about how I was doing and told her how I wanted them to baptize my son and at which school I wanted him to study.

When the paper and the pen ran out, I asked for needles for knitting and sewing. That's how I was able to make a strap for carrying the baby. Later on I learned how to make the straps by hand, using a knotting system that one of the guerrillas showed me. They'd use them as belts or for tying up their equipment. Although it took me awhile to get the hang of it, I was finally able to finish two: one for my mother and one for my son, which I brought with me the day we were freed. I also embroidered a tablecloth, which took a lot of diligence and hours of concentration. It ended up being about two feet long, and I used it when I ate with my son. I'd show it in the proof-of-life video they shot of me in 2003, and I was able to take it with me to freedom.

I noticed immediately how therapeutic these chores were for my state of mind. It's impossible for pessimistic thoughts to take over when the brain is so consumed with a challenging task. Finishing the work also leaves you with that gratifying sensation of having accomplished something, and that always made me feel good. In the end, all those chores I did to distract myself from my harsh reality helped me to grow in a spiritual way.

I also mended my clothes when they needed it, though for some reason this wasn't as pleasing. Perhaps it had to do with the stitches I made being too thick. I imagine it's like painting, when the thick strokes you paint are a representation of how you feel inside. Since I was so unhappy in captivity, my stitches came out terrible. I needed to relax so that they would come out better, and that eventually started to happen. I just didn't have a choice in the matter; I had to maintain the few items of clothes we had. I also had to take good care of the knapsack in which we carried all our equipment and things. All of this was a major lesson for me.

We also liked to play cards at the camps, although it wasn't so easy getting someone to loan you a deck, and sometimes I didn't have it in me to fight. I preferred playing chess or checkers. But if someone loaned me a deck, I'd play solitaire. The three Americans, contractors Keith Stansell, Thomas Howes, and Marc Gonsalves, would loan me theirs every once in a while and taught me how to play Russian Bank with them. (They'd been held captive by the FARC since February 13, 2003, when their plane, on an antidrug mission, crashed in the middle of the jungle—although U.S. authorities contend that guerrillas shot down the aircraft.) The policemen were experts at bridge and taught me how to play. My favorite game, though, was King, which needed four players. But those who played it would sit there for hours, which I wasn't into doing all the time. They also like to gamble the chore of washing dishes, and since I played so poorly, it wasn't worth the risk. In general, the same people would win all the time. I rarely played, and when I did, it was only to socialize a bit with the others.

One of our fellow hostages was a master of the dice and loved to play Parcheesi. We'd play for our breakfast arepa, and that I didn't mind so much. However, the game consisted of running your chips around the board without letting yourself get eaten. This proved boring to me after a while, so I kept the number of games I played with him to a minimum.

Hours and hours of nothing to do eventually led to conversations that would end up in backstabbing sessions about the other people at the camp. As we say in Colombia: "small village, big hell." I avoided getting involved in the gossip, finding it both irritating and mean spirited.

Once in a while, but not as often I would have liked, the guerrillas gave us some books and magazines to read. The comandantes would hand them out to the entire group so that whoever wanted to read them could. I'd swallow up every thing that fell into my hands. When I was in Martín Sombra's camp, there were a lot more offerings, so I spent that year reading a lot. I remember reading books by Jules Verne, Gabriel García Márquez, Enrique Santos, and Vlado, a Colombian cartoonist. I'd eagerly read the magazines from cover to cover, advertisements and classifieds included. There is no comparison to how

I read magazines today as a free person. Usually, I haven't even glanced at the current issue when the following week's edition has already arrived.

I'd often read out loud. I'd sit in a corner and listen to myself. I thought it would be important to know how to read like this, pausing to lift my eyes off the page, just in case I would speak in public again in the future. One time I read aloud, from start to finish, an outdated report about poverty in Colombia; it had to be at least one thousand pages long. Some of the other hostages didn't find my reading so charming. In fact, it bothered them, and they complained to the comandantes. One of the comandantes came over to me later on and said, "Look, Clara, since those people bitch so much, why don't you read in your head?"

I also took up gardening. Once I saved a few orange seeds and put them out to dry. Later on, in a corner of the camp, I prepared the soil and planted them. And right before I was freed, I returned to that spot and saw that several small oranges were growing there, along with an avocado tree I'd planted that grew three feet high. These were the little mementos I left behind.

I took pride in constructing the best campsite I could every time they moved us to a new place. To prepare the soil, we used machetes and digging tools called mattocks when they loaned them to us; when they didn't, we just used plain sticks. In order to avoid the quagmires that formed every time it rained, we had to create a system of drain fields in the dirt. Later on I liked to set up a bench and table to eat on. Every time we had to move, I looked forward to a brand new opportunity to redo my modest jungle space.

On average, I'd get my hair cut every month or two. It helped fight the passage of time and, better yet, it kept up my self-esteem. I tried to cut my own hair several times. But when I came out looking nearly scalped one time, I decided not to try it again. There were other hostages and guerrillas who cut hair for the group, and I just decided to go to them instead.

As incredible as it may sound, during the last two years of captivity, the women were given beauty supplies to use, including eye shadow and nail polish. I thought it was important to take advantage of them, especially the nail polishes, since I had always liked keeping my nails well manicured. One of the last nail polish colors they offered us—I will never forget—was frosty gold. I liked it because at night I could actually see my nails glowing in the dark. There was another thought that passed though my head, too: that if all this should come to a tragic end, the sparkly polish would help someone identify my body in the rubble.

18

Motherhood

Colombia wasn't aware that I had given birth in captivity until early 2006, when journalist Jorge Enrique Botero broke the story in a book titled *Últimas noticias de la guerra* (*The Latest News from the War*). He couldn't deliver too many details or confirmed facts and decided that the best thing he could do for his story was to announce that he was publishing the report with a hint of fiction. Here's an excerpt of a quote that Botero gave *Semana* magazine: "Clara Rojas's son is a walking reality that's two years old."

From that moment on, unfounded information and rumors swirled around the media, with different accounts of what could have happened. They were published in all the major newspapers and magazines, as well as some books.

Some tried to reconstruct the story based solely on speculation. They talked of a big drama and love story that had unfolded in the jungle. The only truth in all of this is that I had a child in captivity. That's a fact. All the rest is hearsay.

It's for me to decide what should go public about my story and what should not. And what I've decided is that it's something I'll keep until my son, Emmanuel, asks me about it one day. The only thing I will say is that during my captivity I underwent an experience that left me pregnant. But the actual love story for me began after I discovered I was pregnant and decided to save this baby's life.

My grandmother is the kind of woman that in Colombia we call a *raca-mandaca*: someone with character, courage, and conviction. She had a saying, one of many, that stuck with me despite my youthful age at the time: "It's better to go pale one time than to be discolored your whole life." Or another one that went, *"A lo hecho, pecho."* "Face up to what's done by giving it your chest." Yes, a woman's chest or a mother's breast. I decided to add a marginal note to my grandmother's saying in order to begin the story that transformed my life.

In August 2003, Ingrid and I were told to pack up our things for a trek deep into the heart of the jungle. Without any indications of where our new campsite would be, we were simply told to follow the guerrillas. Our days were interspersed with arduous hikes and long boat rides. The only thing I had brought with me was a backpack, and though I had packed light, it still felt like a pile of bricks. Luckily, the rest of my things—like my mosquito net, the hammock, my clothes—were transported by our captors in a large canvas. Sometimes we'd stay a few days in one place and then continue on.

The trip was a tough one; I was feeling fatigued, lonely, and nervous about where they were taking us. To make matters worse, I was suffering from a powerful bout of diarrhea, and in the mornings I'd awake with such a bad case of urinary incontinence that I almost couldn't make it to the bathroom. This was the state I was in for the entire two-month trek.

Finally, in mid-October, we arrived at a camp headed by Martín Sombra and his boss, Mono Jojoy. It already contained a sizeable group of hostages, and when we joined it totaled twenty-eight military men and ten civilians. We were forced to stay there for a number of months. In the middle of the jungle, the guerrillas had built a large camp with two enormous metal cages that resembled prison cells—one for the uniformed men and the other for everybody else.

Once we were in our cage, we amicably greeted our fellow hostages. Though some were seasoned politicians, I hadn't personally met any of the people in the cage with us, nor had I heard their names before. I was surprised that Ingrid hadn't either. We then extended our hellos to the uniformed captives across the fence.

In each of the gated spaces where we were being held, the FARC guerrillas had constructed barrack huts made of wood, with barbwire fencing in between for ventilation. Our hut had five bunk beds, and I had to sleep on the top bed of one of them. There was poor lighting in the hut, and going up and down the ladder each time took effort, especially when I was a good ways into my pregnancy. Looking back, I'm surprised that I never fell down going to the bathroom in the middle of the night.

At first there was a certain distance between us and the other hostages; a cordiality where I felt that they were keeping their real thoughts to themselves. Despite this, every so often we'd discuss the news or some current event that had made its way to our ears. On rare occasions, I even played cards or chess with some of them. But I spent most of the time reading. There were books at this camp, and I wanted to take advantage of the opportunity to read them.

Months went by at the new camp, and I continued feeling sick. Then I noticed that I had started putting on weight. The idea that I might be pregnant began running through my mind, and I told a few of my hut mates, who advised that I speak to the guerrillas. Since they were the ones responsible for my kidnapping, they were the only ones who could do something to help me. The other captives were right, but their detached response gave me the feeling that they didn't want to get involved, preferring to look the other way. It left a bad taste in my mouth, and it made me feel very alone.

A few days later I requested a meeting with Martín Sombra. He called for me one afternoon after lunch, and two guerrillas took me to his location. On the way, I spotted a large meeting space for conferences and a dining hall that could sit at least two hundred people. I walked into a warehouse type of building, half of which was taken up by a storage facility filled with sacks of what I presumed to be food. Martín Sombra was sitting in front of a computer, with a cabinet on one side of him and a six-foot-long map of Colombia on the other. When he saw me, he stood up and offered his hand. Despite his corpulent build, average height, and hard face, Sombra makes an impression on you.

He invited me to sit and asked that they bring us some bread and coffee with condensed milk. Since I had just eaten, I wasn't hungry. Then he asked, "What's all the fuss about, Ms. Clara?"

"I'm worried that I might be pregnant," I told him bluntly. The comandante immediately summoned a nurse, who must have been around twenty-five years old and was stunningly beautiful. When she looked at my stomach and just kept quiet, Martín Sombra asked her to fetch a pregnancy test. He told me to fast the next morning so I could supply them with a urine sample and that he'd send someone to get me. I was surprised by how he took care of the situation; his demeanor was almost clinical, like a doctor's, without the slightest interest in who the father might be. On my way out, he handed me two packets of wafer cookies and two cans of condensed milk.

That night, I couldn't sleep a wink. I was restless, and it didn't help that the guards had a habit of loudly opening and snapping their rifles shut in the middle of the night as a subtle reminder that they were armed. I'll never forget how the following day, September 18, 2003, Sombra had someone come for me before seven in the morning. I had my urine sample ready, and they escorted me to the same place I had been to the day before.

The comandante and the nurse were waiting for me. We sat down at a table, then she handed me a pregnancy test strip. I poured a small amount of urine over it. According to the test kit's instructions, red indicated positive, and, sure enough, little by little it began turning that color. A chill coursed through me, and I felt my eyes welling up with tears. Naturally, I was happy; having a child is an important part of a woman's life. But to give birth in the jungle? I felt too scared to offer my chest to the situation, as my grandmother would have expected. How was I going to face up to this?

Before the kidnapping, I had thought seriously about having a child. The idea of being a mother and starting a family was something I'd always aspired to do, but for one reason or another, I kept putting it off. Now, as the realization that I was indeed pregnant sank in, I contemplated the other considerations. In three months, I was going to turn thirty-nine, and I was acutely aware that my biological clock was ticking. Despite the medical risks—to both mother and child—of having a baby while being held captive in the jungle, I immediately discarded any thought of not having the child. This could be my last opportunity to become a mother. And besides, under ordinary circumstances, I wouldn't have thought twice about going ahead with the pregnancy, so why would I allow my present circumstances, while less than ideal, to change that?

The nurse and Martín Sombra congratulated me and tried to show their support. He recommended that I apply jaguar oil to my stomach when I wasn't feeling well. The guerrillas extract this oil from the large felines they hunt as a remedy for all types of aches and pains. In fact, on several occasions, the comandante sent a female guerrilla to rub it on my belly for me.

I pleaded with him to take me out of the jungle or at least send me to a medical center nearby, which I knew could take days to reach. I told him that I was a city girl, close to forty, and that this would be my first child. "I will be putting my life and my baby's life in danger by having it in the jungle," I said resolutely, adding that I didn't think I could handle it. Seeing that he wasn't going to grant either request, I begged Sombra to at least allow Red Cross International into the camp to assist the birth. I was completely stressed. On my way out, the comandante attempted to cheer me up.

"Clara, don't worry yourself too much," he said. "We're not going to let you or the baby die. And remember: that baby is yours, and you're going to take care of it like a furious tigress."

When I got back to the barrack hut, I found that the majority of my fellow captives were waiting to hear the test results. And it emotionally affected them almost as much as it did me when they found out I was pregnant. We had spent only a few months together, however, and, in reality, had shared very little. It would be hard for them to truly take part in what was happening to me and offer the necessary support.

The only person I trusted was Ingrid. But unfortunately for me, she was going through a bad time, in addition to the fact that we had been distant for months already. She never tried getting close to me, though she did help in a few ways, like sewing clothes for the baby. But however you look at it, she didn't come through like a sister, which is what I would have wanted and what I really needed. She also wasn't open to creating a friendly atmosphere so that I could ask her questions about childbirth and caring for an infant, something that I would have loved to do. After all, I was a first-timer, and she already had two kids. The only thing she said to me after I told her I was pregnant and she saw my worry was, "Welcome to the club." The words sounded sarcastic, as if motherhood were some kind of burden. It wasn't like she was inviting me to her rose garden. That cold attitude of hers became, without a doubt, the norm of behavior that the other people in the group adopted as well. Even today, they still hold a certain resentment toward me, thinking that this will help them be in Ingrid's favor and gain them her sympathy.

One morning, the male prisoners set up a trap so they could perform a grill-session on me. I was asked to sit down at the table with them so they could begin their inquisition regarding the identity of my child's father. They told me things like, "If you don't tell us, our families could be in danger," and "You're completely irresponsible." I saw that they were very tense and keen on knowing what had happened. As the popular saying goes, they wanted to know who had "scored" with me. I thought they were pathetic, and I figured they were scared that one of *them* might be the father. Or perhaps they feared, though it doesn't seem logical, that they might be killed because of this.

I remained calm and listened to them, like I usually did. Then I asked them in return, "Is one of you sitting here the father?" One after the other, each of them responded, "No."

"Very well, then, what do you have to worry about? Leave me in peace, and I'll answer for my baby."

Not the slightest bit of concern was shown for my baby, although they did try changing their hostile and ungracious behavior toward me. But there were still traces of it in some of them, so that these types of uncomfortable incidents kept presenting themselves time and again. In any case, it didn't occur to any of them to ask that I be freed so I could give birth in decent conditions or that they move me to the closest medical center. Nobody tried to help or support me during that critical time, despite some of them having veterinary training or having helped out their own wives during childbirth. Their only concern was that if I died, they could be blamed for it.

Some of the other women hostages, despite being mothers themselves, acted as if it was none of their business. They didn't give me a chance to confide in them, something I would have greatly appreciated. Perhaps they thought I acted too independent, and perhaps they were right. I had decided I didn't want to ask anything of them. Even so, when I was far along into the pregnancy, they knitted little baby outfits. But then, one of them flat out declared, "Clara, you don't need medical attention; being pregnant isn't a *sickness*."

Extremely upset by her lack of concern, I responded, "Of course pregnancy isn't a sickness. But it requires medical attention and a specialist. And if it doesn't, how do you explain that each year in Colombia the majority of deaths are linked to pregnancy, and that the highest number of infant mortality cases occur in the first two years of a baby's life? Why deny me the right to live and my child the possibility to be born?"

I spent Christmas 2003 with my fellow hostages. It was unpleasant and sad. My only moment of joy happened at midday on December 24: I was knitting, and so absorbed in my work that I wasn't even listening to what they were saying on the radio—until someone called my name and pointed to the radio. I turned around just in time to hear my brother Ivan's, voice; it had been so long, I almost didn't recognize it. That morning he had gone to Caracol Radio's station to send me this Christmas wish, using my brothers' pet name for me:

"Clary, we're waiting for you. Merry Christmas!"

I got so emotional that I began sobbing. To receive those words from a loved one was deeply moving; I felt so alone in captivity. One of the women came over to me to say that weeping wasn't good for me or the baby. I told her that they were tears of joy, and that this would pass soon enough.

At night, when everyone was asleep, I'd whisper to my baby the nicest things about this world I could think of. Whether it would be a boy or a girl I would entrust God to decide: only He could get us through this. Those were special moments: my little one and I alone together, dreaming about how we would build a better life for ourselves after we escaped the hell we were in. Today, when I put Emmanuel to bed and we pray together, I'm aware that all those moments before his birth were important. They created bonds between us and helped build the path that we wanted and are taking today.

As my pregnancy progressed, the camp's atmosphere only grew stranger and stranger. Apparently it wasn't just me who had problems living with the other hostages. Being caged in that little place was simply too much for a group as diverse as us. We were all on edge, knowing that the Colombian army was getting closer and that at any moment there could be a rescue attempt or a confrontation with the guerrillas—two situations in which we would almost certainly come out losing.

Around that time, the guerrillas had stepped up security and spent their days loading weapons. We were on constant red alert, with government planes flying overhead all day long. Terrified, and in our state of perpetual anxiety, everyone began exploding in anger at the most trivial things. For example, if someone got his coffee before the other, a fight would break out, and more than once we had to calm people down. In my case, things especially took a turn for the worse. Because I was pregnant, I was extrasensitive, so that everything that was said to me affected me emotionally more than it would have normally. A fellow hostage actually suggested that I forget about the baby and hand it over to the guerrillas, and that I should invent a fictitious father for the child. I was under the impression that a lot of the others didn't want to see me freed for the birth, and on some occasions, their intolerance bordered on cruelty. I later learned that some of the gamblers in our hut had actually wagered bets on whether or not I would survive.

Such was the situation that Comandante Sombra decided it would be best to separate me from the rest of the hostages. When it was time to say good-bye, there was a lot of drama, at least for me. It wasn't as if I owned a moving van's worth of possessions, since the FARC hadn't replaced all of my equipment after my escape attempts, but my duffel bag still weighed a lot for someone about to enter her third trimester. Only one of my hut mates offered to help me carry it to the door. Others wandered off to the bathroom to avoid having to say good-bye, while still others couldn't be bothered to get up from their seats or put down their cigarettes long enough to bid me a decent farewell. One of the few to come over to me was crying as if I were on my way to the guillotine. It was pathetic. When I finally reached the gate to the outside, I chose not to look back. But I walked out of there with a determination to survive, and to do so, I had to go through all that I had.

Analyzing the situation now with distance and time, I find it almost laughable, in terms of how ridiculous human behavior can be. But I suffered enormously through it and underwent moments of such severe tension that I was putting my life and my baby's life in danger.

19

Emmanuel

My move to solitary confinement took place in late January 2004, when I was close to six months pregnant. They moved me all the way to the opposite side of the camp, near the post exchange, where the guerrillas kept all their supplies. Close by stood a barn with a pair of large pigs inside and, alongside it, a corral with about a hundred enormous field chickens. That's where they had decided to place a spacious barrack hut with a canvas over it for me. It was big enough to fit a bed, a table, a chair, and some boards to put my things on. Off to the side of it was a small wash basin made out of a pair of trash cans, a hole dug in the ground for garbage, and another hole for toilet usage. After having shared such dark and narrow spaces with the other hostages, this hut, with its private bathroom, felt like a luxury suite. I immediately fixed it up and organized my things. The boards I'd sleep on were so wide that it was like sleeping in a king-size bed.

I soon discovered that I had been allocated a particular area for walking and drying out my things in the sun; I couldn't go near the post exchange or the chickens and pigs. A guard in charge of the animals wouldn't let anyone by. At night a female guerrilla would take over the day guard's shift. She liked to stand about fifteen feet away from my hut so that every time I had to go the bathroom, I had to ask her permission. On top of that, I had three other women guerrillas in charge of me: a nurse who came every evening at six, a woman who came at four in the afternoon to make sure I had enough water in the trash cans, and another who was in charge of bringing me food. I hold fond memories of the three, since I could sense that they truly worried about me and gave me as much attention as they could. Though they limited themselves to doing what they were told, they still had a good attitude about it. They weren't overly sweet, which was perfect for me. I preferred to maintain a somewhat distant relationship with my captors.

It wasn't long before I established a new routine: I'd wake up around four in the morning, go to the bathroom, brush my teeth, and light a small candle. They'd given me a bag full of candles that I made last as long as I could. Next I'd sweep and leave everything in order just as the sun was starting to rise, which was the time I liked to pray with my rosary. I was without a radio again, and I missed hearing the news. Sometime before six, I was brought bread, powdered milk, and a thermos of boiling water for coffee. Each week they'd give me a bag of bread, and I'd eat one slice a day every morning. Afterward, I'd rest until eight, pray with my rosary again, walk for about a half hour, wash my clothes, and then tidy up.

The rest of the morning I spent sewing diapers and baby clothes. I used the sheets they had supplied me with and an extra towel I had managed to put away. I'd get hungry very early. Luckily, I was one of the first to have lunch because as soon as the food was ready, the female guerrilla would bring me my meal. Since it was rare that I'd finish everything on my plate, I'd ask permission to bring my leftovers to the pigs and entertain myself a bit. Around one in the afternoon, I rested and prayed again. Then I would walk a little more, and, taking advantage of that private bath, I'd wash myself again. At four they'd bring me my dinner, which usually consisted of an agua de panela with *cancharina,* a wheat flour puff pastry. When I finished, I'd wash the dishes, so that before five o'clock I'd already finished all of my day's activities.

I had plenty of space and time for myself. I no longer had to tolerate strange noises or deal with someone smoking near me. There was practically complete silence all around. Though I did miss the radio, I enjoyed that tranquility *and* having a bathroom to myself, which relaxed my nerves a lot. Nobody could bother me, and I didn't miss the other hostages at all. During that time, I knew nothing about how they were;

the guerrillas who guarded me did not mention them, nor did the guy who came to clean out the trash cans. And apparently they hadn't attempted to send me a message either.

But there were still sounds all around me. From my hut, I could hear the noise that came from the bakery—even this camp had one—every time they turned on the gas to make the bread. Sometimes I could hear a distant couplet from someone who was singing and playing guitar. The sound of the wind: that's what bothered me most. It would rustle the trees' branches and cause them to make a frightening wailing sound right out of a haunted forest. It grew to be so nerve-wracking that I asked if they would cut a few branches.

Another sound generated a different type of anxiety. There was a period when every day, throughout the mornings and afternoons, I could hear the sound of army planes and helicopters circling the jungle. I was always careful to bring in the clothes I had hanging out to dry, especially the long-sleeved red shirts I had at the time, which would have caught their attention. I was certain that the army was very close by, and the more I tried to stay calm, the more the noise would exacerbate my fear that a dangerous military operation would be triggered. In fact, according to Colombian journalist Jineth Bedoya Lima's book *En las trincheras del Plan Patriota (In the Trenches of the Patriot Plan)*, the army squadron that was tailing Mono Jojoy knew that I would soon have my baby and had already located our camp. Later on we found out that the army had managed to get to the camp after we had already abandoned it. (The Patriot Plan, launched in March 2004, was an ambitious military operation put forth by President Álvaro Uribe, with economic backing from the United States. It attempted to force guerrilla commanders out of the jungles by placing Colombia's army in remote areas of the country where guerrilla enclaves are located.)

Realistically speaking, I had a lot of things against me: the risk of an imminent military operation, the lack of emotional support, no news or message exchanges, no doctor in the camp, and no chance of getting proper medical care. The thought of escaping occurred to me more than once. I thought that the first level of security guarding me would be relatively easy to sneak by, and it wouldn't be hard to reach the creek, which had to eventually lead me to the river. But then I realized that the river was constantly being traversed by guerrilla boats. I also wasn't sure how I'd carry my food and all the things I needed for the escape. I was thin; I hadn't gained more than ten pounds during the whole pregnancy. I knew that carrying all of those supplies and starving myself wouldn't be good for the baby, either. The thought of being in the middle of the jungle and going into labor prematurely in my seventh month also held me back. There were just too many obstacles, so I abandoned the idea. Later I found out that no more than seventy feet away from my hut, more guerrillas were standing guard in case one of us tried to escape. I never would have made it. In total, the camp had more than two hundred guerrillas on site.

The situation was so out of my control and the load I was

carrying so overbearing that I decided to trust in God. One fine day I said to him, "I want to live, dear Lord. I put my baby's life, and mine, in your hands." From that moment on, I stopped all the worrying. Deep down I still had hopes of being freed or that they'd bring me to a medical center or at least allow a Red Cross doctor into the camp. I paid close watch to all the boats coming in, thinking that perhaps one was coming for me. Up until the last moment, naïve me actually thought that one of these wishes might come true.

During those last three months before my baby was born, I began performing positive visualization exercises. First I decided to concentrate on what I was going to name him. Since I read the Bible from start to finish, I thought it would be nice to give the baby a biblical name. Emmanuel came to mind because it held a special meaning: "God with us," which is a blessing, and that's what my son would become for me. There's a passage from the Old Testament—I can't remember if it's in the book of Psalms or Proverbs—that says that blessings and curses make up the two sides of a coin, so that everyone chooses which side he or she sees. And I chose to see my son as a blessing from God. I even decided to give him a compound name to honor the two men who made a difference in my life. His second name would be Andrés, after my father, and the third name, Joaquín, after my grandfather. So if I had a boy, I decided I would name him Emmanuel Andrés Joaquín, and if it was a girl, Clara Sophia—Clara, after my mother and me; Sophia, after the goddess of wisdom. My daughter would have to have been very wise to survive in such a harsh environment.

From then on, the blessings began to enter my life. Despite all the potential dangers, I was calmer. There was peace in my soul. Telling myself that I wouldn't be the first woman to give birth in the jungle or in the middle of the woods put me at ease as well. And I remembered the story of what had happened to the wife of the man who took care of my parents' country house three hours outside of Bogotá. She was pregnant and went into labor while her husband was out plowing the fields. Since it was a remote village, she couldn't yell for help. Her four-year-old son, who was with her at the time, was able to find a kitchen knife to cut the umbilical chord. I was ten at the time, and I would always remember how cool and calm she was while telling us her story. It left a deep impression on me.

It's important to have the appropriate role models in life for the moments you need them most. And she became one for me during this worrisome time. Each day I thought of her and would say to myself, "I also have to be able to do this." With all of this self-convincing, my attitude improved tremendously. My appetite started waning again, and I wasn't eating much. But luckily my weight and sleeping habits were fine. The exercises I did every day, along with my bathing rituals, kept away any physical discomforts or infections during the pregnancy—except for my swollen feet, which all pregnant women suffer from. I alleviated the problem by lying down and keeping them elevated. It not only relaxed me but also allowed me to build up the energy I'd need for later on.

That's how I spent those months leading up to mid-April 2004, when I was due to give birth. On Thursday, April 15, I woke up thinking that if my baby were born that day, it would share a birthday with my grandmother, and that would be a nice coincidence. I spent the morning doing my usual activities, and after lunch, when I started sweeping my hut, I felt my first contraction. The person who cleaned out the trash cans had come by and asked me how I was doing. I told him that it was almost time and that he should go tell the comandante and the nurse and remind them that they had promised to send a doctor.

A little while later, the nurse arrived and told me to lie down. I asked her to please bring me a watch to begin counting the frequency of the contractions. That's when a male nurse arrived to tell me that he'd be assisting me, since there wasn't a doctor at the camp. He told me not to worry, that he had studied medicine, though he'd never graduated from medical school. Naturally, I started to cry. Those brutes didn't have a thing ready and, to top it off, no doctor. "May God protect me," I screamed inside.

From then on, the nurse, the female guerrilla who brought me my food, and the male nurse stayed close by and never left my side. Then in paraded a group of guerrillas who I had never seen before; they said they were there to help and remained outside of the hut. When it started to get dark, they lit a bonfire and started roasting some meat while they talked about Lord knows what. My contractions were still going, and I had no appetite.

Out of nowhere, the male nurse asked, "Clara, have you ever left Colombia?" I told him that I had. With an eager look on his face he replied, "Then tell me about a certain trip that you took." I thought about it for a moment and told him about the time I went to Venice, Italy, when I was twelve. And I spent a good chunk of time reminiscing about that. I remember that night as a special one; with all those people outside the hut, offering me a different kind of company, telling their stories and jokes beside the bonfire, which they left burning all through the night. Sleep finally overtook me, and I remember sleeping intermittently until sunrise.

My contractions continued at the same rate. I hadn't eaten in several hours, and I was feeling weak but with no desire to eat. Around nine in the morning, the male nurse and the two women guerrillas tried to see if they could help me give birth naturally. I couldn't do it. They even got a cord to tie from one side of the hut to the other so that I could stand and hold on to it while I pushed. The nurse told me that if the situation stayed the same, a cesarean birth would be necessary—we'd wait until noon to see. If by then there was no sign of the child, they would give me general anesthesia and open me up to save the baby.

I begged him to do me a favor and make an effort to save me as well. He laughed and said, "Clara, don't worry. Hopefully you'll give birth naturally, and we won't need to perform a cesarean. In any case, I also have to ask for authorization to perform the surgery. So we'll decide at one o'clock what to do."

By noon I had already lost a lot of amniotic fluid and noticed that my contractions had started to slow down. We all thought that the baby was suffering, and I noticed that the guerrillas were now concerned. It soon became evident that a cesarean would be necessary. It was impossible to grasp the fact that I was in such an extreme and dramatic situation: in the middle of the jungle, on the verge of a cesarean section, and without a medical team. There was nothing more to do; I was left in the hands of God. If it was His wish, I'd die. And if He wanted it, my son and I would survive.

The nurse began to sweat and stepped outside to rinse his hands and splash some water on his temples. He was able to get a pair of medical gloves and arrived with another guerrilla to install a lightbulb that was connected to an electric generator. It was incredible having a bare 100-watt bulb shining over me in the middle of the jungle. That's where I was when one o'clock came and went. Then one thirty. Then two o'clock. And still no trace of any preparations for the cesarean. When it occurred to me that perhaps the nurse had lost his nerve, I screamed, "Either you start now or we both die! . . . I can't feel the baby anymore! . . . For God's sake, start now!" Right then another guerrilla arrived to inform him that they had authorized the surgery. He finally took my arm, looked for a vein, and injected the anesthesia. As the sleep came on, I thought about my *mamita*, my baby, and hoped the end result would be how God wanted it. Seconds later I was in a deep sleep.

When I awoke, it was already night. There were several people around me, but I couldn't see them very well. It was as if they were in another dimension. Someone was holding my right hand to control the flow of the IV and anesthesia. The lightbulb was still glaring over my stomach, and the nurse was sewing me up. Toward the back of the hut, I could make out another woman standing there with something in her arms. I couldn't tell what it was, but I could see that it was wrapped in the sheet that I had sewed. I knew it had to be my baby. The room was completely silent, and the woman was totally engrossed in my child. I tried to sit up and ask about my baby, but they yelled at me not to move. I had catheters all over me, and the nurse told me to calm down.

"Clara," he said smiling, "you're a trouper. Your little boy came out in one piece and is doing fine. Stay still until I finish sewing you up." The effect of the anesthesia was starting to wear off, and I began to feel all the needle's movements. I was shivering from the cold, and my body was in so much pain I could barely move. Someone shouted to someone else that they should go for more towels and sheets to wrap me in. Then I fell back asleep.

The next time I woke up, it was already Saturday morning. I was extremely sore, and every movement was torture. A nurse came over to me and offered me something to drink. I asked her about my baby, and she said, "He's beautiful. He came out with some scratches on his chest and head, and there's a little bruising on his left arm. But he's fine, and those scratches will go away fast. What you have to do now is rest." I asked her why they couldn't bring him to me, and she told me to relax. She said, "They'll bring him over later, after they finish changing him. Now drink this agua de panela to warm up a bit."

Then I asked her why I was in so much pain. "The operation lasted many hours," she explained, "and it was difficult taking the baby out because you showed no signs of life. That's why he came out with his little arm twisted. Your entrails came out, and they had to be put back in." I also lost a lot of blood during the surgery and came very close to dying.

Around nine in the morning, they finally brought me my baby and held him at my side. I cried from all the emotion and gave God my thanks. I never got tired of looking at him. I didn't try to change his clothing at first because it was raining out, and I didn't want him to catch cold. But I could still tell he was a gorgeous child. It was like being in a dream; it was simply incredible. I stared and stared at his peaceful little face and thought about my mother and my entire family and what they would say when they saw him. I was overcome with a wave of intense joy that, unfortunately, didn't last very long. Soon enough the anguish set in about how I was going to take care of my baby in that jungle, especially in my physical state. Once again I pleaded with God to take pity on me.

Not being able to properly baptize my son when he was born, I decided to bless him on my own using the water from the rice. One of the first things I did when I was freed was go to my church and have him baptized so that the Holy Lord could protect him from then on. Today it feels like I'm living in a dream when each night before going to sleep, Emmanuel and I recite the Guardian Angel prayer together.

The two female guerrillas were still at my side; one to take care of the baby, the other to look after me. Later I was visited by the male nurse, who wanted to see how we were. He examined my son, and for the first time, I was able to see my baby's naked body. He was thin, with very long limbs, but his weight and size were normal. Seeing that the scratches on his head and chest were minor made me feel a little better. But what worried me was the future of his left arm. It was feared to be broken just below his shoulder. His little hands looked perfect, though, and he was a beautiful little being. The nurse assured me that the bones in his arm would heal quickly with the help of the right dressing to readjust everything back into place.

Later on he examined me. I was still suffering from harsh pains, and my wound felt very inflamed. He told me they were waiting for a special medicine, an antibiotic that would prevent the scar running vertically over my lower abdomen from getting infected. Powdered milk had also been ordered for feeding the baby, since I still hadn't been able to lactate so that I could breast-feed my son.

So for those first few days, Emmanuel lived on agua de panela, which they fed to him by soaking a cotton ball with the liquid and putting it in his mouth for him to suck. By the second day, they also began to feed me, although I was so ill I couldn't hold anything down. I lasted like this for four days, ones when I also couldn't stop the shaking. The weather turned cold, and it rained a lot. The baby was freezing, so they moved us to another site on the camp where they made leather goods; at least that structure had a wooden roof, doors, and windows. The place was a lot cozier and right next to the clinic.

I was getting worse every day, my belly was still very swollen, and I couldn't eat. By the sixth day after having given birth, I was reduced to a bag of bones. And since the powdered milk hadn't arrived, Emmanuel wasn't getting any better, either. Martín Sombra visited us one day, accompanied by the male nurse.

"You have to eat or you'll die," he told me. "The only way to stop that medicine from sucking you dry is to eat. Here's some chicken soup; at least soak your lips with it. The medicine and the powdered milk have already arrived. Now you have to do your part and stay alive. Remember, your son needs you."

For a whole month, I had to avoid any movement and survived on intravenous nutrition. I suffered from high fevers until they were able to get a vaccination for yellow fever and inject me with it. My son also received a shot of it along with an injection of vitamin K. I can still remember his terror and how much he bled. There was a lot of tension at the camp that day because everyone knew that the army was very close by; the nurse could hardly keep his hand steady while injecting my baby. But little by little, I felt myself getting better. I ate a bit of white rice, some broth, and sipped some agua de panela.

Since I couldn't move, they hung a small hammock for the

baby diagonally from my bed. This way I'd be able to look after him and give him a push now and then to keep the hammock in motion. Emmanuel was growing fast, finishing all his bottles of milk, and his wounds started to heal as well. The first time they bathed him was an unforgettable moment. A heavyset female guerrilla with light eyes, who must have had some experience in this, was sent to do the task. They brought us some trash cans filled with warm water and a pair of chairs so they could sit and wash him by the foot of my bed.

With the baby around, every moment of the day was a novelty. And I wasn't the only one who thought it. Emmanuel became a breath of life in the midst of all that fear of death. We were all aware that we could die at any moment, but his presence filled our days with hope and brought out the best in people.

The camp's medical clinic was right next to where I was staying. Every morning, there would be a line of guerrillas waiting outside for the medicine they needed. When they saw us, they always said hello. Most of them were young men and women. While I was amazed at how young they were, they were taken with my courage when they spotted my son.

As the baby continued getting bigger, each day I felt a little better. I was so absorbed with my little one that I began to ignore the constant noise of the army's helicopters. On a mission to locate us, which was like trying to find the proverbial needle in a haystack, they had begun flying over the camp more frequently. At any moment, we could be discovered.

I spent May 9, 2004, Mother's Day, with my month-old son.

By then I was able to move around a little bit more and was thrilled to have him by my side. By nightfall, the helicopters had begun flying very low over the camp. The female guerrilla in charge of me came in, wrapped Emmanuel up in a very thick blanket, and said tersely, "Clara, get ready, I have to get going now with the baby. The nurse is on his way for you. In a little while, we'll all be meeting on the edges of the camp. Don't worry, all the female guerrillas will be traveling in the same group with you and the baby. And the other hostages will also be evacuated."

My face must have registered my panic, since it was un-usual for her to offer any explanations when issuing an order. She insisted that I get ready fast and offered me my child once more to give him my blessing as tears streamed down my face. It felt horrendous to be separated from him. Then I heard a stampede of people running to escape the campsite. It was the guerrillas rushing out with their rifles and equipment over their shoulders.

Minutes later the nurse came for me. I tried to walk as slowly as I could while grabbing onto his arm. They hadn't taken out my stitches, and I was still very weak. The scar on my abdomen was about eight inches long, and, up until that point, I had taken only a few steps here and there. Now they were asking me to walk at least five hundred yards. Night was upon us. I held on to the nurse with one hand and held the flashlight in the other. Once our trail down the camp's floor-boards came to an end, we began trudging through the mud.

That's where I fainted from the pain and exhaustion. Luckily, I didn't lose full consciousness, although I came to feeling very dizzy. Two of the guerrillas picked me up and carried me a few more yards. Then they placed me on a piece of black plastic sheeting and dragged me along while I held on to Emmanuel. It was such a relief to have him back in my arms. The sky was pitch black, and they ordered us to remain quiet. Up ahead you could hear the clanking of chains on the other hostages as they passed by. I later found out that they were holding them farther away outside the camp. They left me there awhile until finally the helicopters sounded like they were heading off into the distance. Martín Sombra and another comandante—whose name, I think, was Alberto—saw that their people needed a rest and gave the guerrillas permission to light up their cigarettes. It was curious to see all these tiny, glowing red dots contrasted against the blackness of the jungle. Later on they brought us back to the leather goods shack, and we were finally able to rest. But when we got back there were few people around and it felt as though the entire camp had been abandoned.

The next morning, everything seemed like it was back to normal. Several young female guerrillas came by to see Emmanuel and offer us their company. The Colombian army was still nearby. Some of my stitches had opened the night before, so they had to sew me up again, but this time with no anesthesia. What a test of strength!

When Emmanuel was forty days old, the comandantes decided that it was time to take the two of us back to the camp with the other hostages. Though I was still weak, my stitches were already out, and I was able to walk. The move meant that I was going to have to care for my baby all on my own now. But that didn't worry me as much as the environment we'd have to be in. Who knew how my former fellow hostages were going to receive us?

20

With a Baby in the Camp

On June 6, when Emmanuel was already a month and three weeks old, I woke up early to tidy up, though most of my things were already packed up for the move. I dressed my son in his best outfit. Just a few days before, I'd received a duffel bag with all kinds of baby items in it—even disposable diapers, which came as a total relief. I was informed later on that Mono Jojoy himself had personally sent all those things.

Martín Sombra's wife came to say good-bye to me. She was young, fair skinned, and very attractive. Although she had always been cold and distant, on this day she came to say that I should take good care of my son. She had been confined to bed around the same time as me, due to her having fallen on a hike while she was a few months pregnant. Sadly, she lost her baby. She came to visit Emmanuel and me a few times during those forty days. Life has its twists and turns, and over time you start discovering things that seem almost too incredible to be true. After I was freed, I had a few opportunities to visit Martín Sombra—in jail. Colombian police had captured him on February 26, 2008. The first time I saw him, he asked me how my son was.

"Martín," I said, "by sheer fortune, my son and I are together again, but you must have heard about what had to be done to his little arm. The boy suffered."

He answered, "But he's alive and with you. If you only knew how many women wanted to keep him. Even my wife insinuated it, but I wouldn't hear of it." I don't know why he told me this. I kept my words brief and said, "You're right. Thank God my son Emmanuel is alive and with me."

The truth regarding this comandante is that I hold conflicting memories of him. Even before my son was born, I believe that Sombra could have freed me, sparing me from this next painful chapter. He declined to hand me over to Red Cross International or to allow a member of the organization into the camp to assist me—allegedly because of direct orders from the FARC secretariat. However, I do have to recognize that he was the person behind moving me to an isolated place when the tension at the other camp was getting cutthroat. During my labor, he sent a group of guerrillas with experience in both nursing and cow birthing to help out. They tended to me the best they could, despite having the most basic of resources on hand. After I gave birth, the comandante came to ask me—

practically beg me—to eat and assigned me a female guerrilla to care for my son. So I'd say he's one of those types of characters in life who every so often feels like doing something humane for a change.

At nine in the morning, the male nurse came to take us back to the place where my fellow hostages were being kept. I had my expectations, but I felt calm and satisfied. After all, Emmanuel and I had gambled with our lives and won.

When we arrived, I was surprised to see that they were all gathered together at the entrance, singing me welcome songs. Afterward, I was told to go to my former barrack hut and sleep in the same top bunk as before. When I got to my bed, the men began to ask the guerrillas in an angry tone to accommodate me and the baby in a more comfortable place. They had already envisioned how complicated it would be for me to climb up and down with a baby all the time. Though their intentions were good, the manner in which they asked didn't get us anywhere, so I just went to my place, fixed it up, and left Emmanuel on the bed so I could hang up his little hammock.

When I was close to being done, the rest of the hostages came to tell me they were going to start a hunger strike to insist that the guerrillas give me a better place. I told them it was fine with me if they went on strike, but that I couldn't because I was still too weak. The whole episode was kind of funny because then they decided to celebrate our arrival with a fermented agua de panela they had stored and start their hunger strike the following day. But the concoction ended up not sitting well with most of them, and they were hit with a bad case of the runs the following morning. Even so, it was still like a day of fasting.

As the government army's threats continued to escalate, the high stress level at the camp was palpable. Every day it seemed like the planes would fly lower and lower, and what drove us insane was not knowing what would happen if the army landed. Would the guerrillas be given orders to flee the site? Or to kill us all first? Our captors were visibly nervous, on alert and with their weapons loaded. We felt trapped in that overcrowded prison, with nowhere to walk to. It wasn't like the other camp they'd sent me to, where I could walk to calm my nerves. They never let us out of the large cage, not even to go to the bathroom anymore, since they had built one inside the barrack hut. The hut was so narrow, we established a system of taking turns to walk around in it, being that it was impossible for all of us to move about at the same time.

Going back to that terrible place with a newborn baby made it worse, and we quarreled about everything. Emmanuel cried when he was hungry or cranky, like all babies, but his cries resonated in the camp and more so when there was silence. Since I didn't feel comfortable asking anyone for anything, I watched over him night and day, feeding him, washing his clothes and mine, while trying to stay alert. I rationed the disposable diapers and used the cloth ones during the day, as the male nurse had advised, but I had to wash them four times a day.

I woke up early one morning because my son was crying, but after a guerrilla brought him his feeding bottle, he fell back asleep, and I took advantage of the time to wash some clothes. Just as I was close to finishing, I heard him crying, dropped what I was doing, and bolted back to see what was wrong. I calmed him down again.

When I got back to the wash, I was met by some of my hut mates complaining that I hadn't picked up my clothes or straightened up after myself for the next person. In general, they treated me as if I were a stranger to that camp. They reminded me of the type of fussy people who stay at five-star-hotels and immediately call to complain when they find the slightest detail out of place. I found it all ridiculous, and I was tired of fighting with them. So at the entrance to the wash room that day, I just stood there choosing to stay quiet.

Another time they complained to the comandantes because I had bathed twice in one day. I did it because I had been washing diapers and felt totally drained, and since it was already late afternoon and everybody else had washed, I thought I'd take a quick rinse to wake me up. They found it horrendous and began saying that I got too much leeway. At that moment, I was approached by one of the three Americans, who said in his rudimentary Spanish, "Don't worry, Clara, I just kept quiet. All this complaining seems like a big exaggeration over nothing, and I don't want you to be upset."

The comandante, who was sick of these fights and how childish the hostages could act sometimes, said, "Look, we brought Clara and the baby here with you because we thought that they'd be better off. But you haven't helped, and it looks like you don't want to, either. Go now, we'll figure out how to resolve this." This resulted in the male nurse coming to me the next day to say that they were going to take my son for one month. In that time, they intended to cure his arm so that it would attach correctly to his body, and in order to do so, he needed to be completely still and kept calm. The female guerrilla who had looked after him before would be in charge. I was destroyed by the news and was sure that the real reason they were going to separate us was because of all the disputes between me and the other captives.

That's how it went: the nurse came and took Emmanuel. I almost lost my mind when they snatched him from me. I started getting up very early so I could walk before sunrise. I specifically asked for the first turn of the day so that I could exercise and sing to the Virgin. Some of the other hostages would whistle to me to shut up, while others just stopped talking to me. It was incredible: after having provoked this situation, they acted as if nothing had changed.

One day I clutched onto the barbwire fence and shouted desperately to the guerrillas to give me my son back. I called them bastards and lowlives, though those were the least impressive examples from my long line of insults. My screams must have reached the edges of the entire camp; even Marulanda, miles away in another camp, must have heard them. Each scream was followed by complete silence on the camp site, except for the echo of my voice. Afterward I had to apologize to the male nurse and promised I would never do it again. But as the saying goes, "Paris is well worth a Mass," and I was willing to do anything to get my son back.

Around that time, a few of the military and police hostages from the adjacent hut began offering me their solidarity by sending over embroidered gifts for Emmanuel. They made a diaper bag, a blanket, and some two-piece sweat suits that looked like they could have been store bought. Sometime later I received a hand-sewn stuffed owl, and a pair of rattles and a baby mobile that they'd built themselves. They were even able to make leather sandals and the smallest pair of sneakers I've ever seen. I was deeply touched by each and every beautiful gesture, especially because, in comparison to the rest of our hostage group, they came from the humblest of backgrounds. That's something I'll never forget.

To fill the void that Emmanuel had left, I tried to keep myself busy knitting again. But my anxiety interfered, and I could no longer just patiently wait for them to return my child to me, so I decided to start another hunger strike. I offered myself to the Virgin and did not eat for nine days. The male nurse came to tell me that in my fragile state, starving myself was insane. I was aware of this, but I felt that I had to do something drastic, not sit there stoically with my arms crossed until they brought him back to me.

The protest worked. A few days after I completed the fast,

the male nurse told me that they would allow me to see my baby again, but only for a few hours a day. They still wanted to avoid any more scenes with the other hostages. After a month of being separated, I finally got to see Emmanuel in late July. I was still very weak, feeling like it was me against the world. But during my times spent together with my son, I tried to be as cheerful as I could. I read him stories, I sang to him, and as time went by, I started growing calmer again. I concentrated solely on taking care of my baby and stopped paying attention to my hut mates and their absurd behavior, choosing to socialize with them only when they came over to see us in a friendly manner. When Emmanuel wasn't with me, I'd ask the female guerrilla looking after him to send me his dirty clothes so that I could wash them. That way each time they brought him over, I'd wash and change him with whatever was fresh or with one of the outfits that the military and police hostages had made for him.

The three Americans, Tom, Keith, and Marc, had been acting friendlier toward me, so I began spending my free moments with them. We played chess and Russian Bank, read books in Spanish aloud to one another, and discussed the news. The chores for cleaning up the barrack hut were divided between all of us. Since I was still weak the first month back and excused from any initial cleaning responsibility, later on I had to contribute and teamed up with one of the Americans to share the duties. Cleaning the bathroom required moving heavy trash cans filled with water, so he took care of that, and

I did the rest: serving the food, washing the dishes, cleaning the table and chairs, and sweeping the floor. He also helped me mop the floor after someone complained that I didn't do a good enough job, and I decided not to even try it again. The other chores didn't bother me, and I felt like I was just another member of the group who had the right to speak up about what else needed to be done. But the truth is, I didn't complain much. Under the circumstances, I found it silly to ask that they take out the garbage or dispose of their cigarette butts. They were very inconsiderate toward us nonsmokers. We had agreed that smoking would not be allowed inside the barrack hut. But there were plenty of times where that rule was broken.

Deciding to completely ignore everyone else's laziness helped me to cope. But as prisoners who lived in a constant state of angst, people began to explode at one another over nothing again. It happened to me one day while I was in line to get hot water for coffee and for sterilizing Emmanuel's bottle. I usually tried to get there first, since I was the only one who had a thermos. The rest had plastic cups, and they preferred to wait awhile before going because the heat would burn through their cups. One day when I was filling up my thermos, Ingrid yelled at me for going first, startling me so that I spilled some water and burned my hand. One of the Americans tried to calm me down and advised that I shouldn't say a word back to her. It seems that after so much time spent together, the Americans were no longer as reserved and felt the need to help. Another one added, "Don't even think of coming here again for hot water." From then on, every day he picked up my water for me.

Today none of this has any relevance. But I was hurt when it happened. Though these fights were over nothing, all of those confrontations soured my mood tremendously. And I'm aware of how I've had to make an enormous effort to get over this and heal these war wounds somehow.

21

The Trek

By September 2004, we had the Colombian army on top of us. Each passing day, its green military planes and helicopters flew lower and with more frequency over our camp, so we all knew that the guerrillas were going to have us flee into the jungle again before the government found our exact location.

My American friends urged me to eat more so that I could get in shape and start lifting weights in preparation for the trek. They resourcefully created a makeshift weightlifting machine by inserting rope through a pair of metal eyes nailed into a tree, then tying the other ends around two plastic garbage cans, like a pulley system. At first they filled the cans with only a little water, so that it wouldn't be too heavy for me. But little by little, they kept adding more water as I got progressively stronger. When we did commence our march to yet another camp, I could walk normally again and carry my own equipment.

My son was only five months old. I packed all his things away and left what I'd need on hand to change and feed him on the road. The same female guerrilla who had taken care of him since he was born was going to carry him along the way. I don't want to write too much about her—since I imagine that she's still in the jungle, and I wouldn't want to do anything that could conceivably put her in harm's way—but she was an exceptional woman. A few days after Emmanuel was born, she came by to see me and offered to take care of him while I was recuperating.

One day she asked me, "Does it bother you that I'm in charge of taking care of your son? I'm worried that you may think I'm too overweight and might not like that."

I was taken aback by her question and her candor, and replied, "Thank you for asking. In general, I don't have those types of prejudices. If the comandante says it's okay, it's fine with me. Your wanting to take care of him is without a doubt the most important thing." To show my gratitude I made a gentle joke by adding, "And I imagine you cook very well and won't let him ever starve." That's how she came to take care of Emmanuel.

One night in late September, just as the sky was darkening, the male nurse came to tell us that the time had come: we'd begin our journey the next day. He asked that we take as little as possible with us. My baby was to go inside the sling that Ingrid had made for him back when I was pregnant. It had occurred to Ingrid that it might come in handy, and she was right. It was a very kind gesture on her part.

By dawn we were all ready to go. We had even managed to clean up the hut and tie up all mattresses as we had found them. There was a certain nervousness among us, and we passed around a bottle of vodka. One of the Americans, perhaps sensing that we could be split up along the way, came over to say, "Let's toast to forgiving one another. I never want to have a problem with you ever again." I thought it was a friendly gesture, though it wasn't the first time he had tried to smooth things over with me.

After that, we said our amicable good-byes to one another and started on our trek. We were a huge group made up of thirty-eight hostages and about two hundred guerrillas. They put me far up in front of the procession so that I could be close to the women guerrillas who were with my son. A few hours into the walk, I no longer had the strength to hold all of my belongings and had no choice but leave behind the bag I was carrying and my mat. On the second stop we made, I got rid of another half of my things because I couldn't bear the weight. I was left with a tent, a mosquito net, a hammock, a change of clothes, a towel, eating utensils, toiletries, and the skin of the huge snake that had turned up in the river more than two years before. On a daily basis, I'd entertain myself with it by putting it out to dry. Despite having gotten rid of almost everything, my backpack still weighed about thirty pounds.

The path through the jungle was tough, but we eventually got used to it. It was without a doubt our most difficult trek because we had the army on our heels and had to move fast. The guerrillas were edgy, and a lack of sleep doesn't help one's decision making.

Every morning they made us get up at five o'clock sharp. At six they'd bring us breakfast. We had to eat fast so that we could wash our plates and pick up our packed lunch for the day. With those extra items to pack, I'd close up my backpack and see if I could handle the weight. Then I'd adjust the straps according to what felt best, comb my hair, and wait for the order to go. I had completely internalized the military rhythm.

Before we headed off, I'd visit Emmanuel, who was up in the front, so I could at least give him a kiss and my blessing before we set off again. Afterward he'd fall right back to sleep. I was positioned to walk behind him and in front of a group of sick persons who either went by foot or were carried by stretcher. Every three to four hours, we'd stop to rest. Since I was already hungry by then and eager to lighten my load, I'd wolf down my food while we waited for the last of the group to arrive. Later on when the rest were eating lunch, I would spend time with my son and feed him. We'd rest after lunch and then continue walking until nightfall.

Once the guerrillas had found the spot where we would make camp for the night, they assigned us our places to sleep. The first thing we did was to hang up our hammocks and then get ready to wash up in the river. I'd wade into the water with whatever I was wearing, so that the river would wash the mud off my clothes. Then I'd go back to the hammock to undress and put on my other change of clothes to sleep in. Around seven in the evening, they'd call us for dinner, but I was usually so exhausted that I'd skip the meal and hit the sack.

We walked for about ten hours every day. The trek was hard on everyone but worse for the military hostages, who moved in pairs because they were chained to one another by the neck. Watching them struggling through the undergrowth was a sad sight; it was like a scene right out of a film about slavery. The chains never came off. And by night they could hardly move a muscle, since an additional set was used to chain them to a tree when it was time to sleep. The three American captives and the women were chained up only once—though there was that time Ingrid and I were chained up after our second attempt at escaping.

In order to ensure a clear path, the guerrillas would always send a small group ahead of the pack to hack away the undergrowth with machetes. They'd also cut tree trunks and place them over brooks for us to cross over. One by one, with all of our equipment on our backs, we'd step slowly across the trunk and try not to lose our balance. If you took one bad step, you and all the weight of your backpack could drop at least a few feet down. And if there wasn't any water, the fall was even harder. For the chained men, this was even riskier, since if one slipped, the other one would get dragged off the makeshift bridge and into the water—by his neck—and surely choke.

One day we were asked to perform a heroic deed, or at least that's what it felt like to me. It was midday, and we had arrived at the bank of a large river about one hundred feet across and very deep. The current was so strong that to attempt it even by boat would have been impossible. So we had to cross over it hanging from a thick cord that they set up extending from one side to the other. At least they didn't force us to cross with our equipment. And because we were also allowed to undress, I put on a pair of shorts. The Americans went first, followed by another woman and then me. To my surprise, we were able to cross the cord, going hand by hand, submerged only up to our knees in water.

From the other side, though, we could see the panic written across some of the other people's faces, especially the ones who didn't know how to swim. My baby was also among the first to cross, tucked inside a little plastic boat that they had prepared; one of the women guerrillas had dragged it along with her. So as not to worry me even more, I wasn't allowed to see how they were going to transport Emmanuel across. That's why when I saw that he was doing just fine—looking like he was on vacation with his clean clothes on—I could breathe again. Afterward, we had to wait some time for the entire group to cross over. Everyone made it, even the ones in chains. Having passed this test seemed like a good sign of things to come for all of us, and I thought that it might mean we all could be saved.

After days upon days of laboring through the dense jungle, one morning in late October, Ingrid approached me with a message. I was surprised, since we were hardly on speaking terms, but she said, "Clara, they're going to split us up into groups." Sure enough, the guerrillas announced that we had the army on our trail and that it would be easier to move in smaller groups. Then they started reading off the names assigned to each group. We moved in to hear better.

I was surprised when they announced Ingrid's name along with various military hostages, all of them men. But I kept quiet. I was reunited with my son, and that's what mattered most. Ingrid and I had spent so much time apart already that it didn't even occur to me, or to her, to request that we be kept together. Later I heard a malicious rumor that Ingrid had asked the comandantes to separate us because she couldn't take me anymore. I didn't pay much attention to it, thinking that even she wasn't capable of being so extreme and that the guerrillas wouldn't pay attention to these types of trivial complaints anyway. When it was time, I went up to her to say good-bye and told her that we should entrust ourselves to the Virgin de Guadalupe. I honestly thought that the guerrillas would put us together again somewhere down the line, as in the past. And when the group I was assigned to with my son headed off, I joined in without a word.

Our group was made of up twenty-six hostages including Emmanuel, the other two women, the three Americans, and the rest were civilians or military and police. We stayed together for a few more days until they split us up again, taking from our group a few of the soldiers and police, whom we never saw again. Among them was police sergeant José Libardo Forero, who'd been kidnapped by the FARC in 1999. I spoke to him for only a few minutes during our time together, but I remember him as kind and generous. I was changing my son when he came over to say good-bye. He gave me his copy of the New Testament and an image of the cross and said, "Clara, may you and your son be protected by this Holy Cross. Don't ever lose heart, not even for a second." I stuck that image of the cross on the back of a photo I had of my child that they had given me months back, and they both came with me to freedom. As of 2010, the married father of two was still being held captive.

Now we were down to eighteen hostages. We continued trekking together until October 31—I remember the exact date because it was Halloween. After months of little to eat and constant hunger, I had a craving for something sweet that day. I asked for a piece of panela, thinking it would be the only thing our captors had, and they ended up giving each of us a whole bar. I broke it into pieces and put it away in a plastic bag so the ants couldn't get to it. Each day I'd eat a piece; this gave me a boost of energy when I was feeling especially fatigued.

A few days later, they told us that they'd be splitting us up yet again. The Americans and a few of the uniformed men would go off on their own. With them went police captain Julián Ernesto Guevara, then in his sixth year of captivity. He was starting to suffer from health problems involving his legs; in fact, on that same day, they had removed his chains because his legs were so badly bruised. Captain Guevara continued to deteriorate and died fifteen months later at the age of forty-one. We heard about it on the radio. According to his fellow hostages, the guerrillas didn't afford him adequate medical attention.

Colonel Luis Mendieta, who stayed with us, suffered from the same tropical ailment as Guevara, among other maladies. The two officers were taken hostage along with 59 other policemen during the FARC's infamous November 1, 1998, assault on Mitú, the capital of Vaupés province. During the three-day siege, some 1,400 guerrillas overwhelmed the city's police force, killing 60 or so officers. As of 2010, Colonel Mendieta, then fifty-two years old, with two daughters at home, was still being held hostage in the jungle.

By November we had a new comandante known only as Jerónimo, who arrived with a group of young guerrillas to guard us. They looked like children to me; they couldn't have been older than fourteen, carrying those rifles on their arms. The new comandante told us that under his leadership, "Nobody's ever going to have to suffer through hunger again." And he stuck to his promise. He was able to get meat, yucca, plantains, and even some vegetables like carrots and tomatoes to eat. He asked that they cook us some soups and a traditional dish called *sancocho,* which is prepared by adding yucca, plantains, potatoes, onion, and some meat to water. In any case, our diet improved greatly, and from that point on, we didn't have to hike on a daily basis but stayed in the same place for two to three days, on average. Around the end of November, we set up a camp where we would stay for two months straight.

22

Christmas

One of the hardest times of the year to be a captive is during Christmas. Especially if you're accustomed to being together with family and friends to share those days with laughter, harmony, prayer, and delicious traditional dishes.

The season starts on the eve of December 7 with a candle-lighting ceremony for the Feast of the Immaculate Conception, celebrated the following day. The Roman Catholic novena, nine days of private or public prayer, takes place from December 16 through December 24, during which time families usually recite prayers, sing Christmas carols, and eat the Colombian dessert natilla and fried round balls called *buñuelos*, made from flour, cheese, and oil. Christmas trees go up and nativity scenes are displayed showing baby Jesus in the company of the shepherds and the oxen. Christmas Eve features a special dinner, and at midnight gifts are given out to the children. New Year's Eve throughout Colombia is celebrated with firework displays, and you'll often spot neighborhood kids lighting sparklers. The holiday season comes to an end on January 6 with Three Kings Day.

Naturally, there's none of this in the jungle. You couldn't find enough candles to brighten up those coal-black nights—another reason you especially miss the warmth of human kindness and the joyful spirit that characterizes the Christmas holiday season. Whether it's the 24th or the 31st, in captivity every day is exactly the same. If there's anything to differentiate them, it's the level of melancholy you suffer.

The guerrillas, on the other hand, aren't as affected by missing out on the holidays. They just don't celebrate them. Who knows? Perhaps they never did. But the fact is that they completely disregard these dates and act like they don't miss a thing from back home. Not even their mothers.

But that first Christmas with my son, in 2004, despite the circumstances, was very special. Around that time, the new comandante had created a more stable environment, and we didn't have to keep hiking from one campsite to the next each morning. And although our nights were spent practically sleeping out in the open air, at least we were better fed. We had a radio to listen to in the mornings from five o'clock until eight o'clock, and after six in the evenings. They had also brought us cards and some extra clothing. My son received a new shipment of disposable diapers, two new bottles, and—I will never forget this—a walker. Emmanuel had already started to sit up, and I'd put him in that contraption so he could roll around and play with the red telephone connected to the table in front of him. That was also useful when I fed him. For his bath, they brought me two bottles of baby shampoo and an oval-shaped green plastic tub. He loved when I bathed him, and I had a ball washing him and having him smell so good.

We could hardly believe it, but that generous package sent to us included a Styrofoam cooler filled with close to fifty ice cream pops, a total luxury in the jungle. When December 1 arrived, I requested permission to cut down a shrub and placed it in the middle of the small area where they served us our food. I invited the other hostages to participate and asked them to save the ice cream pop wrappings, which I turned into decorative balls for our Christmas tree. To my surprise, the four military men and policemen contributed Christmas cards that their families had sent them years back, while others created ornaments and star shapes, so that everyone ended up leaving his or her special mark on the tree. While it was up, the chickens would run around the Christmas shrub, as did a pair of pigs, and Emmanuel would stare in awe at the sight of it all. In case of a military attack, he was still taken to sleep in another location with the women guerrillas. This way, they would be the first to evacuate and more likely be able to save his life. Comandante Jerónimo was at least generous with the amount of time I could spend with my son. He would send him to me early in the morning and allow me to stay with him until dark. Usually this allowed for us to eat all our meals together and enough time for me to prepare a bath for him before he left.

When the week of the novena started, we prayed together in the mornings and sang carols in the evenings, accompanied by the rhythm from the maracas that one of the policemen had made to liven up our songs. At one point, the comandante gave our group two small white chickens and a cock. The police were in charge of taking care of them, and by the end of December, the most adorable chicks were born. The face that Emmanuel put on when he saw them! Having animals around relaxed us a little. All these elements helped to make that Christmas a lot more enjoyable than most in captivity. The only thing that dampened our good spirits was the news that one of our fellow hostages had lost a sister. All of us could feel his pain.

●

23

The Long Separation

Sometime in mid-January 2005, an insect bite left Emmanuel's left cheek infected. The nurse cleaned the wound and covered it with gauze so that it would heal better. But after a while, I noticed the infection spreading and getting worse. What's more, it seemed to be stinging him, because he cried and tried to remove the gauze that we reapplied after his bath. I began to worry and said something to our new male nurse. He was young and good natured but, in my opinion, very inexperienced; his idea of adequate supplies didn't include bandages or even Band-Aids.

Since the bite still wasn't getting any better, I went to Comandante Jerónimo. After hearing about Emmanuel's symptoms, he said, "It might be leishmaniasis," an infection caused by a parasite and common in tropical jungles. The condition causes skin ulcers and requires longterm treatment with intravenous infusions of an antiprotozoal agent called Glucantime. Like any infection, if not treated promptly and correctly, it can be life threatening.

I asked if they had the appropriate medication to treat leishmaniasis and took advantage of the moment to complain about how my son's malformed arm wasn't receiving proper medical attention either. The comandante explained that Emmanuel needed the pediatric version of Glucantime—he couldn't be given the adult version.

"We don't have it," he said flatly. The only way to get a hold of the drug was to order it from outside of the jungle, and that would be too dangerous, given the army's proximity. When I heard this, my heart raced and I replied, "And how long will it take for the medicine to arrive? My son can't wait! Why don't you hand him over to Red Cross International so they can take care of him and take him to my mother? You know very well that this is no place for a baby. I need to save him! You just said yourself that the army is near, and I don't want to even imagine being in the middle of a military operation with the baby.

"You're going to wind up looking like a bunch of barbaric guerrillas for exposing a child to this," I added bitingly. "We managed to keep him alive through the most difficult of moments; you can't just let him die now."

A few mornings later, I was showing Emmanuel a flock of baby chicks when the comandante approached us. "Your son definitely has leishmaniasis," he said. "We're going to take him for fifteen days so they can administer the medicine, and afterward we'll bring him back. Is this okay with you?"

Without giving it much thought, I said, "Of course, I'd rather be able to take him myself!"

"That's impossible, and you know it," he snapped. "If you're spotted by anyone, we'll be fucked. Be prepared to say good-bye to him on January 23, the night of the full moon. That night we'll transport your son." I pleaded that he at least be taken by the kind woman guerrilla who had cared for Emmanuel since birth. But this made him angry.

"Shit, you're some stubborn broad!" he yelled. "Nobody can be seen! Not a hostage like you, and definitely not one of the guerrillas! The boat will come to pick him up."

Filled with dismay, I went back to my hut and tried hard not to cry in front of Emmanuel. But he seemed able to sense that something was happening. One of my hut mates came over to ask me what Jerónimo had said, and I told him that they were going to take my boy, give him medicine for fifteen days, and bring him back. "And you said *yes*?" he asked with a look of surprise. I told him that I had said yes so that the guerrillas wouldn't try to get out of taking responsibility if the baby got worse. They could put the blame on me later on by saying that I didn't allow them to take Emmanuel for treatment.

From that moment on, I tried to make my baby's days' special and enjoy every moment with him. When I read to him, he'd listen quietly. One time I lit a candle and looked for a passage in the Bible about faith. After I read it to him, I added some of my own words that came straight from the heart:

"Emmanuel, my son, you're still too little to understand, but I want you to know that above all, your mother loves you. You're the light of my life, and Almighty God will bring us together again. You have to have faith and be assured that's how it will be. They're going to bring you to another place, and I won't stop thinking of you until the day I see you again. Go in peace knowing that you are not alone. I, my son, love you more than anything. And despite being so little, you have shown special qualities that have come from somewhere. Remember that I love you, you love me, and that we love each other. Conjugate that verb always."

I blew out the candle and kissed him and hugged him tightly. Emmanuel laughed, thinking it was all a game, and I was happy that he wasn't aware of what really happening. I promised myself I wouldn't cry or make a scene when they came to take him away. This would at least make it easier for him.

January 23 arrived, and at ten in the morning, they sent him to me already washed and dressed in a new outfit: a pair of jeans and a T-shirt. He was barefoot; he didn't have any shoes that fit him anymore. We spent the entire day together until sundown, the time the guerrillas said they'd come. I had already said my good-byes to him in private, so when it came time to hand him over, I did so calmly. This way Emmanuel would think it was like any other day and not an actual farewell. Around that time, my baby was precious to look at: his hair was light, like mine at that age, and I had just trimmed it and saved the pieces, which I still have today. Before handing him to the guerrilla, I gave him a tender hug so I could feel him close. Then I gave him my blessing so he'd be with God.

Later, when it was completely dark out, I heard the sound of a motorboat start up and then fade into the distance. My eight-month-old son was on that boat heading to an unknown destination, at least for me.

When we got up the next morning, I wasn't the only one who felt his absence. Emmanuel was like the camp's alarm clock: the first to open his eyes and let out his burbles for everyone to hear. His departure left a huge void.

I plunged into a state of deep sadness unlike anything I had experienced in my entire life. I spent my days alone, without the urge to speak to anyone, and could barely eat. One morning I began preparing my things for the upcoming move we'd be making to a new camp. I was mending a piece of clothing with a pair of scissors when one of my fellow hostages came over to talk to me. I don't know what he imagined I was going to do with the scissors, but moments later, they came to take the scissors away from me. How I'd miss those things later on. Obviously, they all thought that I was suicidal, when in fact the thought never entered my mind. As sad as I was, I knew that I had to stay alive for my son.

24

Waiting

I entered a profound phase of misery around the beginning
of February 2005, when we had to relocate again. The new
camp was cold and muddy. We also had a new pair of comandantes to deal with, who went by the names "45" and Boris.
When I anxiously asked them about my son, they said that
they had never seen him and had no news about his whereabouts. I found this disconcerting, since up until then all the
comandantes had known about Emmanuel, which had made
everyday life at the camp a little easier. But these two didn't
even know that he existed?

A few days after the move, the comandantes gave us three
radios: two brand-new large ones for the group and a small old
one for me, in hopes that I'd cheer up a little. Though it was

a shortwave radio that didn't pick up as many stations as the other two, it did help ease some moments during that uncertain time. My wardrobe was back to the minimal: a uniform for the day and an extra set for sleeping. And I wasn't able to have them get me a deck of cards, a chess set, or any other board game with which to pass the time, either. All I had to get me through each day was the New Testament and a small book on the evolution of man that one of the other hostages had given me. At that camp, there were no more deliveries of notebooks or sewing thread to write or knit my sorrows away.

Because I was feeling so down, I maintained a rather distant relationship with the other hostages, never forming a special friendship with any of them. To be honest, I preferred things that way, so as to avoid any added problems that being in captivity with others can cause you. I just couldn't find the strength to attempt to get closer to them. I limited myself mainly to saying hello in the mornings and at meals. And that's how things remained for the most part, except for those times when we had our differences.

The humidity at the camp was oppressive. What's more, we were near a river, and every time it rained, we were inundated with mud. To avoid flooding while we were asleep in our hammocks, I dug channels on the sides of the hut. To combat the draft, I used the little bit of thread I had left to try patching up holes in the tent left by those killer ants. But that didn't help much. So I asked the comandante to bring us a canvas to shelter us a little better from the fierce wind, or else we'd end up developing lung and kidney infections from the cold. We were all still recovering from high fevers and malaria, which are common in the jungle. When we had some kind of digestive problem, for instance, all we could do was to take an Alka-Seltzer, and that was it. I tried walking one hour every morning and in the evening, but despite my attempts at keeping active, I still suffered from that bone-chilling dampness.

The day came where we were offered new provisions. Our meals began to come with either an *avena* or a *maicena* (cornstarch) beverage, and when I noticed that there was also powdered milk, I asked the comandante if they would prepare us some rice pudding. I figured the calcium would do my bones some good, since I hadn't had any milk after Emmanuel's birth. He had never heard of rice pudding; the poor thing probably never had a mother who made it for him. Despite the fact that half the ingredients were missing, I gave him the recipe anyway. They ended up making it for us more than once, using either sugar or panela for sweetening. Even though it wasn't very good, I really began to miss my mother, because she prepared her delicious rice pudding for us every New Year's. It didn't hold a candle to my mother's, but somehow it brought me closer to her.

February 23 marked the beginning of my fourth year in captivity, and on that day I heard my mother on the radio. Listening to the faint signal fade in and out, I became emotional listening to her talking about how she was taking good care of the fruit trees that I had planted at our country house a month before my kidnapping. Her story took me back to those days, and I remembered how I toiled the earth with a strong desire to reconnect with my roots. My mother's message to me that day reinforced the strong bond we've always shared. After her segment, they read an article that had just been written about her in a newspaper.

Later on I told Comandante Boris about it. He was second in command and stayed close to the guerrillas on surveillance duty. Sometimes I would go over to him and tell him about the news I'd heard—though that meant speaking to him from at least twenty feet away; the normal distance the guerrillas on guard kept from us. Somehow, telling him the news about my family and how they were suffering in my absence made me feel better. He never responded once to what I was saying, but at least he looked mildly interested.

One time I asked him for a newspaper, and he just started laughing. The rebels couldn't understand why it was so important for us to want to read the news instead of listening to them on the radio. But eventually they brought us two popular Colombian magazines to read, *Cambio* and *Semana*. The issues were somewhat out of date, but I didn't care; I read them in their entirety. What I liked most about them was that they covered a broad range of subjects: politics, health, economics, and even food. Sometime in April, Caracol Radio starting airing a new program at eight in the evening called *Hora 20 (20th Hour)*. I loved listening to it and finally felt informed about what was going on in the world. It was like being part of civilization again, especially since I knew a lot of the guests they invited on the show to discuss politics.

Then it was time to change camps yet again. This time they took us to one that was only fours hours away on foot. But imagine our horror when we arrived to see that they had constructed a huge stockade, 180 feet long by 100 feet wide, enclosed by a barbwire fence. It was like being in a maximum security prison. Guards were stationed in two 6-foot-high sentry boxes on its perimeter, and even the barrack hut we slept in had internal barbwire fencing that extended as far as the corridor to the bathroom. There were barbed spikes everywhere, and I was afraid we'd be trapped if there was a flood.

Oddly enough, the bleak accommodations came as a relief to the hostages who'd been chained by the neck. The guards decided that they were secure enough there that the chains could finally come off. For the rest of us, though, it was torture. Our new quarters were so cramped that we could hardly walk around or sleep decently at night. The comandante claimed it was a sacrifice we had to bear, since there was no other alternative. We would stay there until late 2006—a whole year and a half. It was at that camp where, in late 2005, we received word that one of the hostage's husbands had been murdered. Gloria Polanco de Lozada, a congresswoman and wife of the governor of the province of Huila, was kidnapped from her apartment in 2001 along with two of her three sons. Her husband, Jaime Lozada Perdomo, paid a part of the ransom that was asked to free his sons and they were released in 2004. After receiving threats to pay off the rest of the ransom, Lozada Perdomo was assassinated by the FARC on December 3, 2005. She was destroyed by the news, and we empathized with her sorrow. I gave her a black T-shirt of mine so that she could feel she was dressed in mourning attire.

In May 2006, I was told that my mother and my family had learned that I'd given birth while in captivity. During that terribly long and monotonous period, I awaited news on Emmanuel's whereabouts. Months had passed without so much as a word about him. It had been almost a year and half since I last saw my son.

We were also praying that attempts at freeing us through a humanitarian accord with the guerrillas would soon be reached. The government was hoping to liberate a group of sixty or so hostages—mostly politicians referred to as *canjeables* ("exchangeables") in return for the freedom of imprisoned FARC guerrillas. The FARC demanded that Colombia's government offer it a demilitarized zone for representatives of the two groups to meet and negotiate, but President Álvaro Uribe declined.

That stockade, with its spiky barbwire, created such a hostile environment that new tensions began to erupt. Though we were able to stop several of the fights from getting out of hand, there were a couple of times when the men threw punches at one another. As punishment, the guerrillas would chain them for several days.

In late November 2006, I was relieved when they finally let us out of the cage. The only ones who weren't happy were the hostages who had to be chained up once again. We trekked for several weeks through the dense jungle. Though it was exhausting, I was much happier being in an open space again where you could move around more freely.

Then, when the guerrillas were convinced that the army had lost our trail, they brought us back to that jail cell of a camp where I'd spent the saddest Christmas of my life. Soon enough the army helicopters started flying low over our camp again, sending us into a renewed state of paranoia until they moved us to yet another location by the end of December.

25

Murmurs of Freedom

At the new camp where we spent all of 2007, a huge palm *maloca* without walls and a dirt floor had been built for us. A maloca is a structure used as housing by the natives of the Amazon, notably in Colombia and Brazil. They can be round, or rectangular like ours. It had a wooden corridor surrounding it for walking, and since it didn't have any doors, either, we all felt a lot less trapped. But the chains went back on the necks of the military men, and some of the civilians too. We heard on the radio that a hostage had escaped from another camp during a rescue attempt. A short time later, another policeman had fled to freedom from yet another camp. The comandantes stepped up their security measures and even threatened to chain up the women.

We had an open-air washroom, and I was relieved to discover that they had brought the portable lavatory from the last camp. It felt like we were camping out in the open, but in the midst of some heavy rainfall. As a result, I developed leishmaniasis on one foot, and they had to give me more than thirty injections to heal the wound.

I never stopped thinking about Emmanuel and how I still hadn't heard any news. I prayed to God over and over again, asking Him to protect my son. With April came Holy Week and Emmanuel's third birthday. One day I went into a desperate fit over not being able to see my child. I was in my hammock when, for about twenty minutes straight, I sat up and couldn't stop screaming "Get me out of here! Get me out of here! Get me out of here!" The others stayed silent, and I think someone asked me to try to calm down. The outburst left me in a cold sweat. My T-shirt was soaked, and a chill of devastation ran through my body with the realization that I'd been completely abandoned. The next day, I began a nine-day fast dedicated to the Virgin Mary. It was as though I couldn't take my soul anymore.

I think it was already May 2007 when we heard on the radio that police hostage Frank Pinchao had escaped after nine years of being held captive by the FARC. He was one of the uniformed hostages I had shared a camp with before, though I could hardly remember his face. One morning we were listening to a radio program where he was being interviewed about his kidnapping when suddenly I heard him say, "Clara had a child in captivity, and his name is Emmanuel." He also revealed the fact that I had been separated from my son for more than two years, which exploded into front page news.

Thanks to his public declaration, my mother began a media campaign to demand liberation for me and especially for my son. Just listening to her brief messages, even over the airwaves, filled me with a certain strength again that I thought I had completely lost. I was also able to hear her read fragments of a card that she'd written to Emmanuel:

A LETTER FOR MY GRANDSON EMMANUEL
Bogotá, May 24, 2007
My darling little grandson Emmanuel.
You, my darling child, barely three years old, having just left the womb, with your level of understanding cannot yet gauge reality; you may be in an open-spaced environment, but you're very limited because you're not allowed to leave, they won't let you; while you're taking your first little steps, you'll have no idea of the risks you'll face. That you need your mother, who, with all her love, will not only protect you but will hold your hand and lift you when you fall. So she can guide you and make your path less hazardous. That way she can free you from all the dangers that children like you aren't exempt from. But we've been told that she's not at your side. Can this be true? Can it be possible that she isn't able to protect you? That she can't take care of you? That she can't give you her love like any mother should be able to do? That they have her isolated? And that they keep you apart from her? How is this possible? Is there a reason

to make you suffer, to make your mother suffer? They're also making me, your grandmother, suffer.

I hear that you're very cute, very loving, and that in their own way they want to protect you. All children are very fun to play with at your age; you're trying to find your way in the world, learning how to experiment. That's why you risk the danger of hurting yourself. How I long to be able to protect you! To pamper you! I'd give anything to see you! To hold you in my arms!

I feel a profound yearning. I remember when your mother was your age. She was the prettiest thing at three with that big smile of hers. Those are the moments I'll never forget. I will always cherish her candid smile and take it with me in order to keep remembering her. Those full rosy cheeks, so soft, so adorable. I remember the fountain of little golden ringlets on her head and imagine you, my beloved Emmanuel. I see you as a spitting image of your beautiful mother, who since she was very young brought me and her father so much happiness. As the firstborn girl after four boys to arrive to our home, she was the ultimate gift from God, who we baptized with the name Clara Leticia, which in Latin means "pure joy."

My father picked the name. Perhaps it was because I also brought my parents as much joy as when you, my dear daughter, were born. That's where we got the name from. These times need changing! There are so many changes that need to take place . . . You don't know how much we want

to see you two and hold you tight. We want your freedom,
we want . . . Is it possible?

WE WANT YOUR FREEDOM!

Dear Emmanuel, one day you'll be old enough to read
these lines, and I hope it won't be too late for me to see it.
I hope that you were able to move on but most importantly
learn a lesson from it all. With all my love,

Your grandmother, Clara.

At the end of the letter was an email address for anyone interested in joining my family's effort to free us. The other
hostages grew terrified that the army was going to launch
a rescue operation, but nobody said a word to me about it.
We'd recently found out about the tragedy involving twelve
government officials from the province of Valle del Cauca,
who'd been kidnapped on April 11, 2002. In June 2007, eleven
of them died in a shooting at the camp where they were being
held. At first the guerrillas stated that the deaths occurred during a government rescue attempt, but they wound up admit-
ting that it had been their own security failure. Information
gathered later on revealed that the hostages had simply been
shot to death. The only survivor, Sigifredo López, would finally be freed on February 5, 2009, and he confirmed this version of events. The news hit our camp like a bomb; none of us
wanted to end up victims of a guerrilla panic attack.

On more than one occasion during the month of July,
I heard President Uribe declare to the media that the FARC

should release my son and me. Every time I heard his strong, determined voice say those words, I felt my soul return to my body. I was finally being supported. A brand new feeling of optimism began to swirl around my heart, and my days began to change. Though I never spoke about it with anyone else, I embraced the idea that perhaps my time in captivity was almost over. At the request of French president Nicolas Sarkozy, Colombia's government had recently freed an incarcerated guerrilla. Rodrigo Granda, known as the FARC's foreign secretary, was detained by Venezuelan forces in Caracas and later arrested by the Colombian police. By petition from Sarkozy, who got involved in the Colombian conflict in order to save Ingrid Betancourt, Granda was freed from jail on June 4, 2007. It was a unilateral gesture toward reaching a humanitarian accord with the FARC, where two hundred guerrillas, including several women and a two-year-old child, were also released. These actions filled me with a feeling of hope that continued to grow when a few months later Colombian senator Piedad Córdoba and President Hugo Chávez of Venezuela were named mediators between the FARC and the Colombian government to facilitate the humanitarian accord. I never stopped listening to the news, so that I could follow all the developments of the process. At that point, I had no doubt if there was any smoke, it was because there would eventually be fire.

On December 8, the guerrillas prepared us a special meal for the Feast of the Immaculate Conception: grilled chicken, natilla, and, to drink, *masato*. I interpreted this generous gesture to mean something, and I lit a candle and prayed like I'd never prayed before to the Virgin Mary, begging her for my son's freedom and my own. As the Bible says, "Ask, and it shall be given you; seek, and you shall find."

During those months, I began playing a lot more chess. Given that a lot of the other hostages who I played with were great strategists, my game improved greatly. I had acquired the gift of patience, and being planted in front of that table for a while distracted me from the news, and time went by a little faster. I still walked every day and had started running for forty-five minutes each morning. My appetite came back again too. Even though it was the same food as before, I found that it tasted better. Something was telling me that everything was going to turn out fine, and I recovered my inner peace. One night I dreamed about a sweet reunion with my son.

26

On the Road to Freedom

It was sundown on December 18, 2007, we were washing the dishes after eating, and someone turned on the radio. One of the guards shouted over to me, "Clara, listen! They're saying something about your mother!" I got close enough in time to hear Radio Caracol announce, "The nation's first lady personally called Mrs. Clara Rojas by telephone, and the high commissioner for peace contacted the daughter of Consuelo González." Consuelo, a congresswoman, had been kidnapped on September 10, 2001. I immediately signaled her to come over and told her what I had heard.

"Consuelo," I said excitedly, "you and I are both fine. If these people have called our families, it means they're going to free us!"

"Oh, Clara," she replied, "don't get so carried away!" Surprised at her skepticism, I just started laughing. Then I turned up the volume, and I heard them saying that the FARC had sent a communiqué to the Cuban press agency, Prensa Latina, assuring that they were going to free me and Emmanuel. I jumped for joy and said to Consuelo, "See? You're going to be reunited with your daughters before Christmas."

Nightfall was upon us, and I hurried over to the bathing quarters to try to take in the last ray of light in the sky. I took my time in there, trying to compose myself as well as absorb everything that I'd just heard. I splashed water on my face as if to prove that it wasn't all a dream. When I got back to the hut, the others had already heard and asked me what I thought about it. I told them that we had to wait and pay close attention to news developments because the comandantes hadn't disclosed any information to us yet.

I got under my mosquito net like a lighting bolt, still trembling with excitement. I imagined my mother being told the news, and I asked God to give her strength; she was over seventy-five years of age, and this type of excitement could be too much for her. I thought about my son, imagining what it would be like to see him again, and I asked God for the wisdom necessary to face a situation such as this.

Then the others got under their mosquito nets. Everyone was quiet that night, anticipating what was to come. Around eight o'clock, the news came on the radio again, repeating the same information from before. But this time I was able to hear the FARC's complete message to the Cuban press agency: they were going to unilaterally free me with Emmanuel!

Ironically, this apparent breakthrough was triggered by a breakdown in negotiations toward a hostage exchange. In late November, Colombia had suspended efforts by Senator Córdoba and Venezuelan president Chávez to mediate an agreement between the government and the rebels. The abrupt turn of events ignited a diplomatic crisis between the two neighboring countries. In a gesture of good will toward Chávez, the FARC decided to turn over me, Emmanuel, and Consuelo anyway. Chávez would personally coordinate the delivery operation. The guerrillas were to deliver us to a Red Cross International mission somewhere in Colombia; then we'd be flown to Caracas, Venezuela, to be received by Chávez and our families at the same time.

I was so overcome with happiness that I started to cry. I was finally going to see my son again. I had put away some wafer cookies and decided that I would hold on to them to give to him when I saw him. Then I began to think about what I would bring with me and how to keep it to a minimum. I could already see myself hugging my family, and my great expectations only intensified. Then I fell asleep, with the radio still humming in the background.

The next day, I woke up before dawn and began praying for everything to turn out well. When the sun had peeked over the horizon, I got up to go to the bathroom and ran into Consuelo. She was smiling.

"So *now* do you believe it?" I asked her. She let out a hearty laugh, and I was glad to see her happy. I went back to my hammock. The others were listening to the radio program that sent the hostages messages from family and friends. Many of the callers that day conveyed their regards to Emmanuel and me, and that made me feel good. We were glued to the radio until they brought us our coffee. A couple of the other hostages asked me what I was going to buy my son for Christmas. I can't tell you how this filled my head with glorious thoughts. But I didn't answer their questions. Though they had never said anything, I knew they must be feeling great pain over not being freed as well. So I limited myself to thanking them for their kind words.

It was midmorning, after I had waited for my turn to bathe, and before I knew it, lunch was being served. On the way back from filling her plate, Consuelo stopped to ask me if I had thought about what I was going to bring with me. I told her that I was going to pack very little. By that point, I had already cleared my backpack of the hammock, tent, radio, a deck of cards, extra rope, the New Testament (my only book)—even the snake skin I had taken such good care of. My plan was to leave them with the military hostages. I had also decided to burn all of my journals, before the guerrillas asked me for them. Thinking it would be best to do it sooner rather than later, I built a bonfire as fast as I could. The others ran over to tell me to put it out because it was giving off too much smoke, but by then the notebook pages were charred black.

By sundown, my equipment was ready, and I had managed to give away the few belongings I had. In a duffel bag, I had packed a set of clothes for sleeping, a towel, a lightweight string hammock, and a sheet of plastic to place on the ground. No mosquito net or even dishware. What I did pack was a little bottle of shampoo that I had left for special occasions, a small bar of soap, a toothbrush, and some toothpaste. I also dug up a small mirror and nail polish, thinking that I might finally need it. The straps I had made for my mother and Emmanuel were also carefully packed, along with the proof-of-life message I had written years before.

When I finished, I went up to one of the military hostages and said, "I haven't seen any of you writing. Though they haven't said anything to you, I would recommend having some messages ready for us to bring to your families. You know how these people are. At any moment, they could tell us it's time to leave. And it would be foolish not to have anything ready."

Later on I passed Consuelo. "I bet you're all ready to go, aren't you?" I said, which she found funny.

"Remember, Clara," she pointed out, "these people still haven't said a word to us."

"Rest assured and pray to God that everything works out," I replied.

That night I made sure to get a good night's sleep so that I'd be well rested for whatever lay ahead in the next few days.

The following day was December 20, my forty-third birthday, and one of the happiest I'd spent in a long time. I was radiant with joy. After listening to the messages on the radio, several of my fellow hostages came over to say hello. One even ventured to ask me how old I was. Amused, I responded, "I think that as of today I can reset the counter on my age clock. With just the idea of being freed, I feel younger already." Since he insisted on knowing my age, I added coyly, "Luckily, none of my classmates are here; they dislike it when I disclose our age, especially since I'm one of the younger ones. But for me age is synonymous with maturity."

We all just started laughing. Then someone pointed to another hostage and said in a joking tone, "Well, here's the exception that proves the rule."

It was Christmas week, and we prayed the novena with Colonel Luis Mendieta, as we did every year. Before we finished, several of the other hostages came over to pass on the messages they'd written for their families back home. It was heartbreaking. Every single one of them cried uncontrollably as he or she spoke, and I stood there listening with a knot in my throat. That's where we were when the comandante showed up, calling Consuelo and me over.

"You're leaving right now!" he barked. "Grab only what's necessary! And go right now!" He looked annoyed. Thankfully, I already had my things ready and dashed over to my hut. A military hostage handed me a letter he had written to his mother and son, and I hid it in my things. Then Alan Jara, a former governor of Meta, in central Colombia, came up and asked that I say hello to his wife for him and tell her about his health problems. Alan, kidnapped by the FARC on July 15, 2001, had been suffering from malaria, among other sicknesses. He accompanied me to the door, his face unable to conceal the immense pain he was feeling. I can still see Alan's anguished expression clearly in my mind. (Happily, he would finally be freed, due in large part to intervention from Senator Piedad Córdoba, on February 3, 2009, along with military and police hostages; William Domínguez, Juan Galicia, Alexis Torres, and Walter Lozano; and the politician, Sigifredo López.)

As we exited the hut, many of my hostage mates started crying during the good-byes, while others just stood there mute with desperation. The scene was heartrending, and all the while, the comandante was yelling, "Move it! Seems like you're not in any rush. Move!" Consuelo came up behind me, and I asked her if she'd had time to pack. Yes, she said; everything had been ready to go since the day before.

They took us to a maloca at the camp's exit. It seemed to be a storage place. There was a wood-cutting machine and plenty of sawdust on the floor, along with sacks of chicken feed scattered throughout. We were left to wait there the entire day. In the early evening, a comandante came for us and asked that we turn over the letters that the other hostages had given us to take to their families. It was cruel, but we had no choice but to hand them over or else be submitted to a search. Nevertheless, knowing how hard it was on families with loved ones in captivity, we asked him that they videotape more proof-of-life testimonies with the other hostages. He didn't respond and told us to pick up our things. We were leaving.

We were brought to another campsite where a different guerrilla squadron slept. They brought us our dinner, and afterward, I suggested to Consuelo that we pray a little. I'd asked a guerrilla if they could please loan us a radio so that we could listen to the news; eventually one was delivered to us, and we fell asleep listening to it that night. The two of us wound up staying there until December 22, when low-flying helicopters started circling the area. Thrown into a state of high alert, the guerrillas told us to grab our belongings and that we'd be traveling by foot. Despite my having shed so many items, my backpack still weighed a ton. I threw it over my shoulder and waited.

Soon after, a new comandante arrived and asked us to follow him. I had never seen him before. As we were leaving the camp, we passed the comandante known only as 45. He was with his wife and two-year-old child. I waved good-bye; it felt really good to do that. Through God's help, I wouldn't have to see those people ever again. I walked right past them and didn't get to hear what they said to me.

At one point, my right arm fell asleep from the weight of my duffel bag, and I had stopped to adjust the straps. The new comandante, who I believe was called Isidro, hurried over to me. "Clara," he said urgently, "you have to pick up the pace! We have to get to the boat before nightfall." I rearranged my backpack as best as I could and kept walking, but with great difficulty. I prayed as I went, saying to myself, "This is no time for getting sick or feeling any pain, because I am on the path to freedom." But I couldn't help feeling nervous with the helicopters still whirring above us.

We walked at a good pace for about an hour before finally

reaching the small wooden boat that would take us on the next leg of our journey. Before we'd left the camp, we were given plastic bags filled with white rice and pieces of meat, along with two plantains to eat. We were told to sit on the wooden slat at the back of the boat. It was tight back there, and there wasn't much room to stretch out our legs due to all the guerrillas' equipment. Comandante Isidro and two other men had taken their places up in front when we finally took off around seven o'clock. Since the boat didn't have a roof, we had to endure cold wind lashing our faces the entire trip. But I kept repeating to myself, "Be positive. We're headed toward freedom. Help me, God."

We had the river all to ourselves that night, and you couldn't see a thing. At some point in the middle of the trip, five young guerrillas—three women and two men—also boarded the boat. Though we nodded off here and there, the ten-hour ride felt like an eternity, and we finally reached our destination at dawn.

The next ten days, taking us into 2008, were spent traveling on foot and by boat. Most of the time, we changed campsites every day. To Consuelo's and my growing concern, we never received word from the FARC on how or when they were going to free us.

27

Operation Emmanuel

To our good fortune, Comandante Isidro had brought a radio with him, so we were able to listen to parts of the morning and evening news. We heard that an operation coordinated by Venezuela's president was under way with help from Red Cross International and a delegation of several countries headed by former Argentine president Néstor Kirchner. We heard that even several international journalists and film director Oliver Stone were on the scene waiting to see us freed. All of it seemed surreal to me.

As the days dragged on, I started to worry more and more. We still hadn't met up with Emmanuel, the comandante still hadn't told us what was on the agenda, and I couldn't understand why they hadn't given our coordinates to the Red Cross yet. We were enjoying good weather, with not a cloud in the sky, and it seemed to me that nothing should be getting in the way of moving forward with the operation. The army helicopters were constantly on top of us, and that worsened the tension. One day we heard noises that sounded like bombs and gunfire. We knew it wasn't thunder because the sky was too clear. It became evident that a military operating zone had to be nearby. This at least assured me that we were exiting the jungle and getting closer to civilization, since we had also started seeing houses alongside the river.

That's where we spent December 31, 2007. We ate well that day in comparison to the rest, when fish and plantains were all that we had to eat. The comandante sent someone to go kill some chickens he had received, and since we had some powdered milk, I asked if we could also make some rice pudding to celebrate the New Year. Consuelo didn't like the rice pudding much, but at least she tried it. The sun was setting, and the comandante put on the radio while I was still eating my dessert.

All of a sudden, Consuelo screamed, "No, Clara, they suspended the operation!" I hadn't been able to hear all that she had heard, but still feeling confident, I said, "Oh that's normal. We're all Latinos here, and the festivities await us. They'll go home to spend New Year's, and then they'll resume the operation. Don't worry." With that, I went to the chonto to think more about what she had said. Then I heard Consuelo call me again,

"Clara, hurry up! The president found Emmanuel!"

I ran back as fast as I could and put my ear up to the radio with my heart practically beating out of my chest. I heard President Uribe speculating on what might have happened to my son. It seemed that they had found a boy who had spent more than two years in the custody of the *Instituto Colombiano de Bienestar Familiar* (Institute of Family Welfare), and that it could be Emmanuel. As the president later revealed, a child whose description matched Emmanuel's had been turned in to the ICBF by a peasant almost two years ago. The former police hostage Frank Pinchao's description of the boy's arm had helped them to find him. Uribe later announced that he was going to conduct DNA tests on both the boy and members of my family to verify if it was indeed Emmanuel.

My heart fluttered, and I began to shake violently. I turned to Comandante Isidro and, gesticulating wildly with my hands, demanded, "But how can this be? Weren't you guys saying that you were going to hand him over to me?!" The man said nothing and showed no emotion, as if he really hadn't a clue what was going on. We kept listening until we heard Venezuela's Hugo Chávez speak: "Let's hope, let us hope, that boy is Emmanuel, Clara Rojas's son. Let us hope, hope that it's true!"

His words of concern were greatly appreciated, and I was left hoping that it was true—that my son was already free and that he could be with his grandmother. Consuelo looked at me and asked what I thought would happen now. "It's even easier," I said, "All the FARC has to do is turn in the two of us." But the comandante interjected, "Wait, we still need to hear the results of the DNA tests."

• • •

That New Year's Eve, I went to sleep with my head aching from all the information I had heard. Knowing for sure that Emmanuel had been in the hands of the ICBF all these years would leave me more at ease. There he would have received the best care possible, and it would be easier for me to learn about all that he'd been up to while we were apart. The ICBF was a state-run agency with a very good reputation; it had been established decades ago solely to protect and care for abandoned children.

On the first day of 2008, I woke up early, filled with the hope of now knowing my son's whereabouts. I thanked God for all that was happening and for being able to see my family soon. The radio was playing the song "Caminante no hay camino" by Joan Manuel Serrat, the famous Spanish singer-songwriter, and its lyrics moved me: "Traveler, there is no set path / The path is made while walking it / Blow by blow, kiss by kiss / That's how a path is made." Long after the song had finished, I quietly sang the words to myself.

At six o'clock I heard the sound of our national anthem. It gave me goose bumps, striking such a deep chord inside of me that I stood up and sang along. I was on my way home, returning from a foreign land. Afterward, we listened to the news, and I was surprised to hear that despite the fact that it was New Year's Day, several ICBF workers and Colombian officials had flown to Caracas to take DNA samples from my mother and brother Ivan, who were already there awaiting my arrival. I found it to be a noble gesture that even on a holiday, these government officials were willing to sacrifice their time for our cause.

According to the radio report, it could take anywhere from three to ten days to get the test results. So imagine my surprise when, on January 4, they announced on the radio that a Spanish laboratory had confirmed that the boy in the custody of the ICBF was in fact my son, Emmanuel. This latest development filled me with an indescribable rush of energy and strength.

I felt I was close to my family again. Especially since I could hear them often on the radio telling me that they were waiting for me. Consuelo, on the other hand, remained skeptical. She expressed concern that the guerrillas still hadn't given President Chávez the coordinates to our exact location, and deep down she feared that they had no intention of freeing us. She was a prisoner of her own anxiety, and it got to the point that she even begged the comandante to bring her back to the camp with the other hostages. I couldn't understand her behavior and tried to calm her as much as I could.

"Take it easy, Consuelo," I said. "Think about your daughters and that you're going to see them again soon. It's only a matter of days now. We're so close to civilization already that it would be foolish to take a single step back at this point. Please, Consuelo, try to think of your daughters and your granddaughter, who you'll be seeing very soon." I went to lie down in my hammock and ask the Virgin Mary to fill us both with the confidence that this would all work out. I also asked God to please not let Comandante Isidro pay any attention to Consuelo's plea to go back to the hostage camp. I opted to remain prudent and keep my mouth shut while we waited to see what happened; I trusted that everything was going to be okay, and this helped ease my anxiety. The lawyer in me came out: I awaited all the information, so that I could analyze it word by word and reach a conclusion. But I genuinely believed that the end of our ordeal was close and that we had to be patient and not lose our cool.

We soon started our trek again and came upon a huge piece of farmland; there were malocas with trash cans and farming tools everywhere. On January 9, our hike became extremely difficult as we crossed a huge corn field with palm trees and banana plants. The ground was covered in dry leaves, making it hard for us to step through. There were also tons of mosquitoes circling around, and they gravitated toward our faces. I worried that snakes or scorpions might be lurking beneath us.

We finally arrived at a spot where they told us we'd be setting up for the night. I was exhausted, and my mood darkened when I noticed there wasn't anywhere for us to hang our hammocks. We definitely couldn't sleep on top of all of those leaves, so we tried our best to hang them up close to each other as best we could and remove the leaves beneath us. Although I had a mosquito net that the comandante had loaned me, I was still very uncomfortable sleeping in that narrow string hammock. Since we were close to a creek, the guerrillas asked us if we wanted to wash up. But it was already getting dark, and there was no way on earth I was going to get into that murky water full of spiders and insects; I stayed in my hammock.

Comandante Isidro had hung his hammock about fifteen feet away from ours, and he raised the volume on the radio so that we could all listen. President Chavez was saying, "I just received the coordinates! Tomorrow the FARC will deliver Consuelo and Clara to freedom! Colombia's army will suspend all military operations starting at five o'clock, Colombian time, for ten hours."

I was overjoyed with the thought that this could be my last night spent in captivity. It was pitch black all around us, and I tried to relax so I could get some rest for the big day ahead of us. I tossed and turned until I finally fell asleep. But I woke up several times during the night because, despite the mosquito net, the insects were still managing to eat me alive, and I had bites all over. I kept repeating to myself, "Tomorrow will be a new day, tomorrow will be a new day."

At five o'clock in the morning, I was up and had everything ready to go. I asked permission to wash up, and Consuelo joined me. I wanted to try looking presentable and remove the smell of sweat and jungle I had on me. The creek was in fact horrible, but by day it was a little less threatening. I put on my clean set of clothes and packed everything in my duffel again. Gone would be the days of having to lug that thing around.

They turned the radio on, and I heard my brother Ivan on his cellphone being interviewed on his way to Colombia's San

José de Guaviare Airport so that he could join up with the Red Cross helicopters, pick us up in the jungle, and then accompany us to Venezuela. I was thrilled at the thought that someone so loving was on his way to see me, although in the end, my brother wasn't allowed to board the copters for security reasons. Family members were not allowed to participate in the delivery operations.

Though I wasn't hungry when they offered us breakfast, I ate something anyway, not knowing what the day had in store. Then I brushed my teeth and took a look at myself in the mirror. I looked exhausted, but at least I was happy. I thought about my mother: what would she think when she saw me? And my son, who I hadn't seen in so long: what would our reunion be like?

A few days before, the comandante had assigned a group of about a dozen guerrillas to accompany us. Some would come along with us and another group would stay. We walked for about an hour until we reached a clear esplanade of grass at around ten o'clock. I remember feeling an enormous sense of relief to leave that web of trees behind and gaze up at the open sky. It was a special moment for me, to finally feel the sun's light and warmth on my face after years spent rotting in the jungle's humidity and vegetation.

There we met up with another group of about twenty guerrillas. I got scared when I saw so many armed men dressed in full military attire. Many of them were black and indigenous, with faces hardened by the war. There were also several women in the group, and one of them offered us some water with lemon. We saw that they were preparing flares and gunpowder to indicate to the two Red Cross helicopters our exact location. The sun was getting strong, and they made us stand in some shade near the river's edge to avoid getting badly sunburned.

A little while later, we heard the unequivocal sound of helicopters approaching. I remember my fear when I saw the guerrillas preparing their weapons to shoot up at the air. But Comandante Isidro screamed at them, "Lower your guard!" I thought that the helicopters had flown right past us, and in desperation, I cried out, "Don't let them go! Don't let them go!" I ran out into the sunny field with a white canvas I had and tried to signal the helicopters myself. The guerrillas also started waving whatever they had in their hands while continuing to send smoke signals. The white and red helicopters finally turned back toward us, and I jumped for joy! The comandante asked me to stay still until they landed.

But after the helicopters landed, nobody came out of them. I couldn't understand why they were taking so long to disembark. After a number of minutes that felt like an eternity, a few people with Red Cross International vests began to emerge from the copter. I was so ready to leave that place that instead of waiting for them to come over to me, I ran over to them. That's when I saw Senator Piedad Córdoba, who looked like a movie star, dressed in red with a turban wrapped around her head. I was thrilled to see her. She introduced me to the two people with her: Venezuela's minister of the interior, Ramón

Rodríguez Chacín, who was in charge of the mission; and Germán Sánchez, the Cuban ambassador to Venezuela. They all hugged me hello. I was then asked by the journalists who had come if they could take a few photos and record some images for the world to see. I had no choice but to say yes.

All I wanted to do was get out of there as soon as possible. That's when I saw that the Red Cross members were asking the comandante for a signature to seal the act of delivery. I found the formality a bit excessive; I just wanted to climb into the helicopter and leave that jungle behind. There were tons of guerrillas all around, and I still didn't feel safe. Then the Venezuelan minister handed me a satellite telephone, and on the other end was none other than President Chávez himself wanting to congratulate me on being freed. I could tell that he was also extremely moved, and the first thing I did was to thank him with all my heart for all that he did.

I passed the phone to Consuelo and saw that the minister had begun handing out cans of soda to the guerrillas. The fact that we still hadn't left yet, and showed no signs of it any time soon, worried me. Some of the female guerrillas came over to say good-bye to us. Consuelo gave them each a hug, and before I knew it, I also had them swarming all around me, and I felt I had to reciprocate the gesture. Later on I'd have to listen to all types of conjecture about whether or not we were suffering from Stockholm syndrome, but I told myself that courtesy and valor are not mutually exclusive. We were on our way to freedom already, and we weren't losing anything by being friendly—especially bearing in mind that the majority of our fellow hostages were still in captivity.

When we were finally able to board the helicopter, I was thankful that they gave us a change of clothes and some water for freshening up. Then the other passengers boarded the copter, including Piedad Córdoba, the Venezuelan minister and his wife, two Swiss delegates from Red Cross International, a pair of nurses, and the flight crew. It wasn't until they closed the hatch and the aircraft took off that I finally felt I was free. I was so happy! We were all feeling intense emotions of joy. I was very impressed by Minister Rodríguez Chacín's kindness and how well he managed the whole situation. You could tell that he was breathing easier now that he had us both back in one piece and on our way home.

In the middle of the flight, one of the crew members handed me a pair of headphones so I could listen to the welcome song they had planned for us, which was a big hit in Colombia at that time, by the singer Jorge Celedón: "Que bonita es esta vida" (Oh How Beautiful Life Is).

It was a gripping journey home. I stared at the beautiful scenery through the window, watching how we were leaving behind the jungle in which I'd spent six whole years. We flew for about two hours over green plains until we reached the Colombian-Venezuelan border and the city of Santo Domingo in the state of Táchira, Venezuela.

When we landed, the airport was mobbed with journalists. On the same runway, we changed aircrafts and boarded what seemed to me to be the presidential jet; whatever the case, it was very comfortable. We met up again with the Red Cross officials and the Cuban ambassador, who was a very friendly man. He was eager to talk to me about all things divine and human, and I tried to answer him as best I could, but my mind was so concentrated on my family that I can hardly remember what we talked about. When we were close to landing, Piedad asked me if I wanted to use her makeup kit. I gladly accepted, and I have to say that I greatly appreciated that feminine gesture.

28

The Reunion

When the plane landed at Maiquetía Airport, right outside Caracas, I could see through my window that the runway was filled with people waiting for us. As a result, the airplane steps on which we were to descend were also jammed with journalists. Nervously, I kept looking out the window to try to see who I recognized, when I finally spotted my mother from afar, walking slowly toward the plane.

I was one of the last to disembark, and when I hit the runway, I saw my niece María Camila, my brother Ivan's oldest daughter, engulfed by the throng of journalists. I almost didn't recognize her: when I was kidnapped, she was barely eleven years old; now she was a tall, beautiful seventeen-year-old. We hugged, and she accompanied me over to where my mother was. I was taken aback by how slowly my mother was moving, assisted by a walker as well. Her face could not hide her exhaustion, but I was beside myself with happiness to see her. I thought to myself, "What a true blessing this moment is!"

When she reached me, my mother took my face into her hands just like she used to do when I was a little girl. She looked at me straight on for a moment with those bright eyes of hers and then gave me a welcoming hug that I had been waiting an eternity for. My mother had been told I was dead several times during my captivity. But she never believed them and never lost faith that she'd see me alive again one day.

Hand in hand, we walked toward the lounge they had prepared for us inside the airport. My niece passed me her cell phone, saying that Radio Caracol wanted to talk to me. I was really touched. Though I had just landed in Venezuela, my fellow countrymen were thinking about me as much as I was of them. They gave me a warm hello and asked me how I felt, and it was all very emotional. Then Venezuela's chancellor Nicolás Maduro and other members of his staff came over to say hello, and we talked for a while. And though Caracas's climate is warm, I remember I felt a chill sitting there. I drank a cup of coffee, and they told us that we had to head over to the Miraflores Palace to meet with President Chávez.

A series of cars pulled up for our large group, and we headed toward the palace in a long caravan. Along the way, I spotted numerous people holding banners and signs welcoming me. It was already getting dark when we arrived at Miraflores, and when I got out of the car, the president was standing there ready to give me a kind hug. He told us to proceed down a red carpet they had rolled out for us alongside a line of guardsmen in formation. Inside Consuelo and I had family waiting for us, as well as Piedad Córdoba. I was still very wound up, and my hands were ice-cold; my mother covered them with hers to try to warm them, and my niece brought me another hot cup of coffee.

The president spoke with my mother and me, and we thanked him profusely for his successful effort. The words didn't come close to expressing all the enormous gratitude we felt. Knowing that all we wanted in those moments was to rest and be with our families, he kept the event short. When we were finished, the journalists were let in again to take more photos, and afterward we said our good-byes to Chávez and thanked him again.

They drove us to a spectacular storybook hotel where we had an enormous suite. My brother Ivan was waiting for us there, and he gave me a bearhug hello. When we settled down a bit, my family asked me what I wanted to do now. I told them that I wanted to take a long, hot shower and talk to my son. While I was in the shower, my brother began making phone calls to track down Emmanuel. Under that hot stream of water, I was able to meditate privately on all the emotions I was feeling and relax myself. There were all kinds of shampoos, soaps, and creams to choose from. I must have tried every single one and even went through close to half a bottle of one perfume, which suited me to a tee.

The bathroom had a huge mirror on the wall, and I planted

myself in front of it. I must say it came as a shock to see my entire body for the first time in so many years. In my nakedness, I studied myself: the scar from the cesarean birth, my tired-looking face, and the new wrinkles on my forehead. But I was in one piece, safe and sound, and I thanked God. I exited the bathroom in a white bathrobe and a pair of slippers that were the most comfortable things I had put on my feet in ages. Then I dressed in the new clothes that they'd brought me, along with a pair of stockings and shoes.

Afterward, my mother showed me a large suitcase that had arrived for Emmanuel from the Venezuelan government. It was filled with clothes, towels, children's toiletries, toys, and even a remote control car. The room was full of fresh flower arrangements. This unbelievably luxurious suite even had a menu listing the different types of pillows you could ask for!

My brother passed me the phone so that I could speak to Elvira Forero, the director of the Institute of Family Welfare. She was a very friendly woman, and I was grateful when she went into great detail about how my son was doing. Elvira thought it best that he not be exposed to all the media frenzy, and I agreed completely. But I asked that in any case he be allowed to keep following all the events on television and that we'd talk again the next day. I felt like she was almost a sister; it was such a relief to talk to her. She was so on top of the whole situation that I finally felt I could be at peace.

For dinner we asked them to bring us something light: chicken broth, fruit salad, and ice cream—something I had been craving for some time. Just as we were finishing the last morsels on our plates, Colombia's First Lady, Lina Moreno de Uribe, called to rejoice with my mother, who got on the phone first, and then with me. She was very friendly, and ten minutes later, President Uribe called. In comparison, his tone was cordial and a bit disheartened. I told him something along the lines of how this moment was a time for all of us to rejoice in, and afterward I sensed him less tense. I thanked both of them again for calling.

Though we could have kept talking all night, my family and I thought that we should try to force ourselves to get some rest. I climbed into bed; it was enormous. I melted into those soft pillows and experienced the most incredible delight in feeling clean sheets on my skin again. It was heavenly—nothing like the places I'd slept in for the last six years. I fell asleep right away but was wide awake again at around two in the morning. I went to the window to look outside. We were on a very high floor, and you could see all of Caracas's glimmering lights.

I turned on the television and stopped at a channel with cartoons, thinking of Emmanuel. I flipped through some newspapers and spotted a photo of my son in a Venezuelan daily and then again in the Colombian magazine *Semana*. These were the first images I had seen since they took him away at eight months. He was a four-year-old boy now who had changed so much since I'd last laid eyes on him. I couldn't get over the light in his beautiful eyes. I read the papers until the sun began to come up and then crawled into bed again for a few more hours. At nine-thirty my mother woke me up to pass me the telephone. It was the Colombian radio station W Radio, and I stayed on the line talking with them for more than a half hour.

When I hung up, I got ready and asked the people assisting us if they could call the ICBF's director again to see if I could speak with my son. In the meantime, they brought us our breakfast. Then my brother and my niece arrived, and we began planning our agenda. Later on, a Venezuelan government worker arrived to help coordinate our activities and told us that there was a lot of interest expressed in us holding a press conference. Then he offered us any medical services we wanted and told us that President Chavez had invited us to stay for a month of relaxation outside the city. We thanked them for all their generosity and told him we'd think about it and get back to them.

At that moment, I had two major concerns: reunite with my son as soon as possible and undergo a medical check up. In fact, that same afternoon, a staff of Cuban doctors conducted an initial checkup, including an eye exam. They told me that I needed glasses, which they had ready in a few hours.

The next day, Saturday, January 12, I got up early, and they took several blood tests right at the hotel. Then I went with my mother to a medical center for further tests. We were there until about two in the afternoon and then went back to the hotel to meet my brother and my niece for lunch. He told me that whenever we wanted, the Colombian government would send a plane to take us back home.

I told him that I wanted to see my son as soon as we could. Later that afternoon, we were visited by the Argentine ambassador, who extended an invitation to her country. Then I did an exclusive interview with the Venezuelan network Telesur. On that same night, we decided to hold the press conference. The room was packed; I was taken aback by the large number of international journalists there. My mother and brother sat with me at the table. I opened it up by thanking all the media for following our kidnapping and for their solidarity. Then one by one I answered all the questions that were asked of me. I remember being struck by how kind everybody was and the extraordinary energy in the room. What they were most eager to know was what kind of state I was in and how the other hostages were faring.

When the press conference was over, the doctors were waiting for us back at the hotel. The preliminary test results showed that my health was acceptable but that I should undergo more tests. We decided we would follow up in Colombia so that we could travel home the next day.

On Sunday we all got up very early. I couldn't stop thinking about my son and put on the cartoon channel again to feel connected to him somehow. We went down to the lobby to say good-bye to several people who had come during the last few days to see us. Then a group of journalists accompanied us to the airport. Once we arrived, a Colombian Air Force plane was waiting, and we bid farewell to the Venezuelan authorities. At eleven we set off for Colombia accompanied by two members from the office of the high commissioner for the peace. The young man and young woman, who had been looking out for me since I arrived, were very responsible, and their diligence and caring left an impression on me.

When we arrived over Colombian territory, the captain played the national anthem for us; it was a very special and exciting journey for me, as was my arrival in Bogotá. When we landed, the minister of defense, Juan Manuel Santos Calderón, and the commissioner for the peace, Luis Carlos Restrepo, came on board to receive us. When I alighted from the aircraft, I was met with a podium, a microphone, and the Colombian flag. There were hundreds of journalists filming every moment with their cameras. I was asked a few brief questions and then asked to pass to the VIP lounge. There, awaiting us, was Colombia's First Lady; Bogotá's mayor and his wife; the minister of public safety; San Jose del Guaviare's Council for the Defense of Minors; and ICBF's director, along with other representatives from the institution. I also got to see my other brothers, a sister-in-law, and my youngest niece. We had tears in our eyes from all the emotion. The council updated me on my son's situation and reconfirmed that the DNA tests proved that the boy they'd found in the ICBF's care was indeed Emmanuel.

Later, I finally learned what had happened to my son over the past three years. It seems that on January 23, 2005, or sometime after, the guerrillas had turned over my child to a peasant they knew well, José Crisanto Gómez. He cared for my son until July 20, when he took him to the San José del Guaviare Health Center because Emmanuel needed medical care. The doctors immediately saw what bad shape my son was in and immediately took him away from José in order to give him the medical attention he needed. Today this man is in jail and is charged with kidnapping. Therefore, my son was under the ICBF's care from July 2005 until January 13, 2008, when he was finally returned to me.

From the airport, we drove directly to a northeastern part of Bogotá, where the children's center was located. The minister of public safety and the ICBF's director joined us in the car and informed us on the way there about the medical attention Emmanuel had received during all that time he spent under the institute's care. Thanks to their dedication to keeping the institute's mission a reality and the good will of experts throughout the country, Emmanuel received the care and medical treatments he needed. He had already undergone an operation to adjust the bones in his left arm, and all he needed now was to treat the nerves so he could regain total mobility in his arm. On the way, I also got a call from Attorney General Mario Iguarán, who had also been following the developments with my son and the DNA tests.

When we arrived at the shelter, the center's directors were waiting for us along with other members of my family. They showed us around first, so that we could see the environment in which Emmanuel grew up. I found it clean and well kept. We were told to wait in a small room on the second floor while they went to look for Emmanuel. During those moments, I spotted an oil painting of the Virgin Mary on the wall, and I kneeled down in front of it to say thanks for the most incredible blessing I could ever receive. Then my son walked in the room.

He was stunning, with an intense brightness in his eyes and a captivating look on his face. We stared at each other in silence. He looked so fully formed and grown up for his young age of three years and nine months. They had snatched him away from me at such a young age that to see him already walking and talking came as a shock. It looked like he had recently had a haircut. It warmed my heart that he seemed relaxed and didn't hesitate to come right up to me. I knelt down, and he gave me a hug and called me mommy. This would be the image of our reunion that the whole world would see shortly after.

They brought us champagne so we could make a toast, and Emmanuel joined us with a soft drink. Then my brothers gave him a board game, and, one by one, Emmanuel went around the room so he could meet everyone. When it came time to greet his grandmother, the encounter was also very special. It seems that he had no hesitation when it came to hugging his mother and grandmother because he had already seen us on television. These moments would stay in our hearts and memories forever. Around five o'clock they brought Emmanuel and me to a dining area so that he could eat his dinner. I was pleased to see that he had a hearty appetite and could feed himself his bowl of rice soup. I remember being surprised to see that he ate everything up in a flash, even the beets. Later on he went to the bathroom and flushed the toilet all by himself.

My brother Ivan invited us all to his apartment afterward to see the Christmas tree that he still had up for Emmanuel. When we got there, he had prepared my favorite meal, an ajiaco with chicken. He offered me a whisky, but I passed because I was feeling very tired. After dinner we went back to the hotel, where I'd spend my first days of freedom alongside my mother and son while I organized my new life.

Those days were very special. I remember the mornings, and how the sun's first rays would pour through the room's large window, and I could enjoy watching Emmanuel still sound asleep. After that, my life would undergo rapid changes, and, thank goodness, each new day has been better than the last.

29

Readadaptation

Starting my new life as a mother and getting back to my old routine have been relatively easy. The hard part was adapting to captivity. In fact, I never grew accustomed to living without my freedom. But now, amidst the warmth and understanding of my family and friends, returning to my former life with my son couldn't be a more pleasant and comforting experience.

In a notebook, I wrote down a list of priorities of what needed to get done. And, of course, I had—and still have—a lot of work to do. In captivity I spent many solitary hours convincing myself that I had to stay in the best physical and mental state that I could, so that when I got back to my free life, I wouldn't suffer any posttraumatic stress. I had spent so much time thinking about what my life after captivity would be like—what I would do, where I'd live, how I would educate my child—that I left the jungle with practically a full agenda. I had it so planned out already that I was able to get it all done in no time.

At the forefront was reestablishing a close emotional bond with my son. I wanted to allow Emmanuel the necessary time to get accustomed to me again, while offering him an environment filled with family and friends. The second was to schedule routine medical checkups for my son, my mother, and me. The third was to catch up on the state of my finances so I could decide how to best move forward. And the fourth, which also tied in with my first objective, was to distance myself from the media. A smooth transition back into a normal life was extremely important, particularly for my son.

My relationship with Emmanuel has improved tremendously, but, naturally, it's a permanent and ongoing effort. Today we're very content around each other and have reached a certain level of mutual understanding. We spent the first part of 2008 traveling with the family for a month and half. When we got back, we threw ourselves into taking care of our health issues. Once we had completed all our medical exams, it became clear that we were all going to need surgery, and we planned out our calendars for each one. My mother's operation was the most serious of the three, so she went first. Then it was my turn, though my procedure really consisted of several operations in one so that they could fix the monstrosity of a scar they'd made in my abdomen during the cesarean section and also take out my gall bladder. My recovery was extremely arduous, and I had to stay in bed for a month. But I made an effort to get myself out of bed as soon as I could because we still had to complete Emmanuel's operation on his arm. Luckily, with the help of physical therapy, he recovered a lot faster than we expected. That entire operative period lasted until the end of June 2008, and all the while I was setting up a new home on the outskirts of Bogotá for us.

Emmanuel also started nursery school around that time and he spent his days singing, playing, and enjoying story time. He also turned four, and we celebrated his birthday with his two sets of friends, those from the nursery school and his old friends from the children's home. We also attended several thanksgiving masses at the country clubs my family belonged to and two others at the school and university I attended when I was younger. Soon it came time for Emmanuel to begin his formal studies, and I enrolled him at a school last September.

My kidnapping story piqued the interest of several publishing houses, which wanted me to write a memoir. Sometime in the middle of 2008, after I had returned from vacationing in southern Spain, I finally got down to the business of writing this book. But I have to confess that I went through moments of complete blockage. Going back wasn't easy. And I had to allow myself some time and distance to confront certain things. But for the most part, I found the act of recounting my experience truly stimulating. I've always enjoyed sitting down and writing for hours, and in the future, I'd like to surprise readers by publishing more pleasant tales that don't have to do with being held captive in the jungle.

Throughout this first year, I've participated in marches and several humanitarian efforts seeking an immediate release of the remaining hostages. I've spoken with heads of state, participated in conferences and forums, and on more than one occasion, I've sent messages of hope to both the families and the victims themselves. Naturally, I was filled with joy whenever they freed other hostages, and especially when Operation Jaque was such an extraordinary success. On that mission, launched by Minister of Defense Juan Manuel Santos, on July 2, 2008, the Colombian army managed to free Ingrid Betancourt, the three Americans, and ten other hostages without so much as a single shot being fired. A group of military intelligence pretended to be another group of rebels, arriving by helicopter to transfer the hostages to another site, and fooled their captors, led by the comandante el Mocho César. Despite the friction between Ingrid and me during our captivity, it came as a complete relief to know that she had been rescued and returned to freedom.

30

Time Lost

Sometimes when I look back, I can't help but grow melancholy. There's something I'll just never be able to recoup and that's time. I'll just never get that back. Especially those first three years of my son's life, when they separated us during the most important developmental stage of a child's life. We both suffered irreparable damage. I also lost close to six years that I could have spent alongside my mother and the rest of my family, while growing personally and professionally.

When the FARC kidnapped me, I had just turned thirty-eight and was in the prime of my life. To this day, I still keep asking myself if there's a way to compensate for all that lost time. For former hostages who have been held against their will for a long time, the notion of having been robbed of such a huge chunk of your life can become more painful than the actual hardships suffered in captivity. It's like one day you're just going along life's path, when you suddenly fall into a deep hole. And you're stuck there for years, and your normal life freezes. Ceases to exist. There aren't words to describe the emotional damage.

A few days ago, Emmanuel asked me, "Mom, why didn't you come for me sooner? I missed you."

I answered, "What happened was that certain people prevented me from doing so."

With an insistence typical of youth, he replied, "But why, why, why?"

This time I told him, "You'll have to ask them. But what matters now is that we're together."

Without question, all that pain and suffering left a profound mark on our bodies and on our hearts. But I go on with life and try not to be bitter about my ordeal, treating it as something that just happened to me. Most importantly, neither my family nor I want to go on feeling like victims. That's why since the very beginning, we've made an effort to show on our faces all the happiness we feel to be alive and to have been given the opportunity to reunite and to actually experience a rebirth.

We still have an enormous amount of work ahead of us, and that's to recover as much time as humanly possible.

31

Forgiveness

Since I was freed, I've received countless messages of solidarity and sympathy. They've come in the form of letters, CDs, books, pamphlets, prayers, drawings, and posters. It's in these little things that I've come to realize how many angels surround us on a daily basis with their light and best wishes. But in order to go back to my normal life and adapt to all the changes, I had to first take time to reflect hard on it all, which also helped the writing of this book. As much as I've gone over it in my head, there are still things about human behavior that I have yet to understand. But I've decided to leave all that in the hands of Almighty God, so he can help me, as He did before, with my heavy load.

Life's blessings and curses form both sides of the same

coin, and everyone has to choose which side to see. I'm convinced that if someone harms you, you have to bless them, not curse them. If I plan to move forward and return to having a full life, I have to allow my heart to forgive those who hurt me. And that's what I do, convinced that I no longer want to drag around that painful burden and, worse, possibly pass it on to Emmanuel and future generations. I believe that the best legacy I can leave my son is my transformative life experience. God gave me the strength to get through it. And despite the adversity I had to face, I want Emmanuel to comprehend that his mother is a happy woman. Bearing in mind my son's well-being, I decided to shed any hint of resentment in my soul. I won't let myself be sullen for the rest of my life about something that is now in the past. I have many years ahead of me, and I'm not going to allow this to tarnish them. That entire tragedy is undoubtedly behind us now, reduced to a series of moments, a mere anecdote.

To overcome it, we all need to conjugate the verb *forgive* in all its forms: I forgive, he (she) forgives, we forgive, and they forgive.

32

A New Tomorrow

It shouldn't come as a surprise that I'm optimistic about the future. If there was anything that the whole kidnapping experience taught me, it was to face everyday life with the utmost patience and to downplay difficulties when they present themselves. I feel as though I have completed a mission by writing this book, closing the door on a stage of my life so that I can now open a new one. Still, there were medical matters to attend to in 2009, starting with Emmanuel's physical therapy sessions for his left arm and hand and a hernia operation that I had to undergo as a result of carrying all that heavy weight in the jungle. It was a minor issue, but it still required proper treatment.

There are also new plans that I'm looking into. I enjoy my

role as a mother and want to remain close to my son as much as possible. But I have some remaining free time that I want to fill by doing something constructive. I've received several invitations to participate in international forums and speak about how a person can still have a positive outlook on life after an experience such as mine. Dedicating a few days a year to these types of gatherings would be fulfilling for me. I'd also like to keep writing about topics that concern me, like displaced children, increasing food security so proper nutrition is available in developing countries, and global warming.

I've also decided to remain in my beloved country alongside my family and my people. Despite Colombia's complex circumstances, my country is and will always be a nation of enormous contrasts and enormous possibilities. But while there are challenges and obstacles to face, there's also plenty of passion, spirit, and young people to do so. And with a little help from God, the rest will come for good measure.

Acknowledgments

Thank you, thank you, to all those people who, through the power of their good faith and loving prayers, were able to bring to pass this miracle of life and liberty.

Many thanks to my publishing team at Plon and to those who helped bring this book to so many countries around the world.